THE THREE EPISTLES OF ST. JOHN
and
THE EPISTLE OF ST. JUDE

NEW TESTAMENT FOR SPIRITUAL READING

VOLUME 23

Edited by

John L. McKenzie, S.J.

THE THREE EPISTLES OF ST. JOHN

WILHELM THÜSING

THE EPISTLE OF ST. JUDE

ALOIS STÖGER

CROSSROAD · NEW YORK

2589

1981
The Crossroad Publishing Company
575 Lexington Avenue, New York, NY 10022

Originally published as *Die drei Briefe des Apostels Johannes*
and *Der Brief des Apostels Judas*
© 1970, 1966 by Patmos-Verlag
from the series *Geistliche Schriftlesung*
edited by Wolfgang Trilling
with Karl Hermann Schelke and Heinz Schürmann

English translation © 1971 by Sheed and Ward, Ltd.
The Three Epistles of St. John was translated by David Smith
The Epistle of St. Jude was translated by W. Jerman

Library of Congress Catalog Card Number: 81-68176
ISBN: 0-8245-0132-2

PREFACE

The reader of the three epistles of John has to ask himself, probably before anything else, how two such slender pieces as 2 and 3 John ever found their way into the canon of inspired books. The most likely answer is that a genuine effort was made to collect all the writings which bore the name of an apostle. That these two epistles were preserved indicates how serious the effort was. The first epistle of John is something else; it is larger both in size and in scope. It is also of a quite deceptive simplicity. The reader who thinks that he has grasped it by a superficial reading will be cruelly enlightened if he ever returns to it; and as a result of his enlightenment he may conclude that the piece is beyond his understanding in any hypothesis.

Thüsing here renders an excellent service to the reader. Those who come to the Bible looking for what they believe only the Bible gives are discouraged by commentators who proceed to inform them of problems which would never have occurred to them if they had let the commentators go unread. Not unreasonably they feel that a commentator owes them a solution or at least a rationalization of the problems which he has been so good as to unload on them.

The deceptive simplicity of 1 John is due in part to the simplicity of the vocabulary of John. The Gospel and the Epistles communicate their message with the smallest vocabulary of all the New Testament books. This may surprise readers, who are prepared to accept all they have heard and read about the " sublimity " of the Johannine writings. The alleged sublimity is achieved by the generous use of the key Johannine words which evoke an unworldly atmosphere, words like light-darkness, truth-lie, life-death. When Jesus in the Gospel of John says he is the way, the truth and the life, a sentence is composed which nearly escapes definition but invites to meditation.

Thus it is easy and obvious to say that the theme of 1 John is the commandment of love. It has been said that New Testament morality, which is the morality of love, is easy to understand, however difficult it may be to do. The statement must be qualified by the note that the understanding of the commandment is not without subtlety, although most of the faithful can understand the commandment without the subtlety well enough to know when they are not fulfilling it. John's understanding of the commandment contains such statements as " God is love," a statement quite comparable to the statement of Jesus quoted above. Taken as it stands, the statement is incredible and incomprehensible. It cannot be that, so what does it mean? And again we are led to meditate. We are compelled to ask not what God is—a question we really cannot answer—but to ask what love is; and if we have some insight into love, we have gained some insight into God. Thüsing spends much of his time exploring the Johannine insights into God which rise from this simple, incredible and incomprehensible statement. One learns what love is not by studying either one's capacity or what one owes the neighbor; it is learned by contemplating the love of God revealed in Jesus Christ.

Should not John have gone into some explanation of the ethics of love in practice, as we find in most of the epistles of Paul? It is simply not the style either of John's Gospel or of the Epistles; and it seems that one can say only that this type of ethical decision is left by him to the individual Christian. The anxious person who looks so often for reassurance that he is really doing all he ought does not get much sympathy from John; ultimately, he seems to say, no one can make that judgment except you. And he might add that to ask what you ought to do is less important than to ask what you can do. Love would be defined by no one as doing all you ought. A fear that one has not done all one ought may be really a fear that one has done more than one ought. It is simply a measure which John does not use.

The Epistle of Jude is another of the very small New Testament letters. Stöger has set forth its purpose very clearly. It is a work of some interest in modern times, for it expresses a concern with doctrine not found in most of the New Testament writings. In the modern church doctrine is sometimes given an importance which seems greater than the importance attached to love. That particular type of false doctrine which Jude confutes is the doctrine which liberates the Christian from restraint. In its gross forms this kind of Gnosticism did not last long in the Church. In its more subtle form, which implies rather than teaches that the saved have a standard of morality different from the sinners, it has never died. It believes that those who are basically so good may crowd the rules a bit to keep the wicked from getting the upper hand; Christians may do to unbelievers what it is wrong for unbelievers to do to Christians. Jude did not have such Gnostics in mind; apparently such had not yet appeared. But Gnosticism takes thousands of forms, and because it does it is the most durable of heresies. Its most persistent as well as its most disagreeable form has been Christian arrogance, the attitude which in the Gospels is associated with the Pharisees. The Epistle of Jude is another if less vigorous plea against this.

JOHN L. McKENZIE

THE THREE EPISTLES OF ST. JOHN

INTRODUCTION

Faith in Love

Three primitive Christian documents are included under the heading " letters " or " epistles of St. John." They were probably all written by the same author and, together with the gospel according to St. John, form the so-called Johannine group of New Testament scriptures. What marks them out especially and distinguishes them from the other documents of the New Testament are their conceptual character, their special way of reasoning, and their affirmatory intention. The two shorter letters (2 and 3 John), each of which is only about one eighth of the length of the first letter (1 John), offer hardly anything from the theological point of view which is not also contained in the first letter. The main emphasis of any exegesis is therefore bound to be placed on the first letter.

Many who have read 1 John have come to love it, but it cannot be denied that it is abstract in tone, strange in the impression that it makes, and tiring in its constant variations on the same ideas. This tends to make it difficult to approach, or at least tends to create a barrier to really penetrating study. This serious difficulty must be taken into account in any attempt to explain this letter, which is theologically and spiritually so important and so helpful and which has, with good reason, often been called one of the summits of the New Testament.

Let me indicate three ways in which this difficulty can be dealt with. First, 2 and 3 John certainly amplify the first, more abstract letter in many valuable ways, despite their apparently limited theological content, and they enable us above all to gain a rather more concrete insight into the situation in which the author and those whom he was addressing were placed. Secondly, the attempt has to be made to understand the real meaning of 1 John for Christian theology and Christian life—in accordance with the intention of the author himself. In the third place, the author's thought was above all meditative (as is the " construction " of his first letter) and it is necessary to understand this and the consequences of this specifically Johannine view and of the special character of 1 John for the commentator.

OUTLINE

THE FIRST EPISTLE OF ST. JOHN

The First Part of the Letter
$(1:1—2:17)$

*Introduction to the Whole Letter and to the First Part: The
Proclamation ($1:1-5$)*

THE "PREFACE" (AT THE SAME TIME, THE FIRST EXPOSITION OF THE THEME OF "FAITH IN CHRIST") ($1:1-4$)

Unlike the letters of Paul and the second and third letters of
John, this letter contains no greeting, but begins without stating
who the writer is or whom he is addressing. Instead of this, we
have some solemn sounding and theologically pregnant words to
open the letter. These opening words do not constitute an
" overture " or an " exposition," in the sense that they contain
echoes of all the main themes included in the letter. Love is
not—or at least not directly—discussed here, for example. The
theme of " Christ " is, however, dealt with for the first time—
Christ and his saving work, his significance within the plan of
salvation, and the proclamation of his witnesses. The emphasis
on " testifying " and on the concept " life " shows clearly that
this section of the letter belongs together with $5:4-12$ towards
the end of the third part and of the letter as a whole, a section
which I have called broadly speaking the " testimony of God."
Both sections form together a framework or a pair of brackets
within which the rest of the letter is enclosed. The concluding
sentence of this opening section ($1:4$) corresponds to the sentence
which occurs towards the end of the letter ($5:13$). The writer's
intention and the aim of the letter are stated in both.

What were the ideas that the author wished to put forward in this opening of his letter? His statements can be classified in three groups:

(a) Statements with Christ as the subject: " That which was from the beginning, . . . the life was made manifest."

(b) The perception of the event of Christ by the witnesses (statements made in the past tense): " Which we have heard, which we have seen . . ."

(c) The present testifying and proclaiming (in the present tense): ". . . [we] testify to it, and proclaim to you . . ."

[1]That which was from the beginning, which we have heard, which we have seen with our own eyes, which we have looked upon and touched with our hands, concerning the Logos of life— . . .

The mystery is consciously stressed in the very first words of the letter. The person who is meant from the very beginning is not yet named—not even the masculine is used, but rather the neuter " that which was from the beginning." (This can also be translated as " what has existed since the origin.") It is not immediately clear exactly what is meant by this " since the beginning." Is it since the beginning of creation, since the absolute beginning and origin of all creation, which is the Father himself? We must, however, bear in mind the special character of 1 John, which is less interested in limitations of time and more concerned with God as the primordial foundation of light and of love revealing itself to mankind. The reality in question here goes back to eternity " before the foundation of the world " and is derived from the eternal primordial foundation of God's love.

The same reality is given another name at the end of this verse, where it is called the " Logos of life." Although the mysterious way of speaking is kept up, the reality referred to is not formally equated with (divine) life, the literal wording being " concerning the Logos of life." This " Logos of life " is similar to the personal Word of divine revelation in the prologue to the fourth gospel, the " Word " in which God himself is disclosed. It is the " Word " which, through the revelation of " life "—the fullness of divine life—gives life. More correctly, it is the " Word " which can give life because it contains divine life within itself.

2. . . . the life was made manifest, and we saw it, and testify to it, and proclaim to you the eternal life which was with the Father and was made manifest to us— . . .

This staggering claim can only be meaningful if the Logos really " became flesh," as the author of the fourth gospel says in his prologue. Clearly, the author felt such an impelling need to make a confession of faith in the incarnation here that he had to break off the normal structure of his sentence, leave it unfinished and insert a new sentence in the middle. The " becoming flesh " of the Logos referred to in John 1 : 14 is the revelation of divine life. The very realistic expressions used in the preceding verse— " We have seen with our own eyes . . . and touched with our hands "—make it unmistakably clear that this " manifestation " was not the appearance of a spirit, but the " coming of Jesus Christ in the flesh " (4 : 2).

3. . . . that which we have seen and heard we proclaim also to you, so that you may have fellowship with us; and our fellowship is with the Father and with his Son Jesus Christ.

This verse forms the conclusion to verses 1 and 2. The witnesses are not proclaiming a philosophy or ideas; they are proclaiming

what they " have seen and heard." Now, however, the aim of
this proclamation is stated. What we should expect here is, more
or less: ". . . so that you may have fellowship with God [or,
Christ]," but, instead of this, we hear first of all, to our surprise: ". . . so that you may have fellowship with us," that is,
with the witnesses. For their part, the witnesses have " fellowship with the Father and with his Son Jesus Christ." The
sequence of ideas in verse 3a/3b means that it is only possible,
in the opinion of the author, to achieve fellowship with God via
fellowship with the witnesses. Finally, the person who was
meant from the very beginning is at last named here: Jesus
Christ.

⁴*And we are writing this that your joy may be complete.*

The aim of the proclamation was stated in verse 3; here, what is
stated is the aim of the letter. But are these two aims so very
different? Clearly, the author regarded fellowship with God as
a source of joy. If proclaiming what they " have seen and
heard " and writing the letter bring about fellowship with the
witnesses and, via this fellowship, fellowship with God, then
they also bring about this " complete joy." What is obviously
meant here is that the joy—the great joy—that God intends
Christians to receive is realized.

TRANSITION: THE PROCLAMATION "GOD IS LIGHT" (1:5)

⁵*This is the message [" proclamation "] we have heard from
him and proclaim to you, that God is light and in him is no
darkness at all.*

A transition is provided by this verse. The key word " procla-

mation " or " message " (another possible translation) connects
this verse to the preceding passage 1 : 1–4, while the contrasting
concepts " light " and " darkness " serve as an introduction to
the passage which follows and which would not be completely
intelligible without this introduction.

What does " God is light " mean? Is it a statement about
God's being? It does at first seem to be this, especially if we
interpret it as a gnostic of the period would interpret it, namely,
that God is the substance of light. Or is it a statement about
God's " moral holiness," namely, that God is without the
slightest stain in the moral sense? This would certainly seem to
be the case, to judge from the passage that follows, drawing, as
it does, conclusions for man's moral conduct from the statement
about God in verse 5. Or is it a statement combining both of
these? This is the consequence that we should have to draw if
we were to do justice to both views.

To what extent, however, do we have the " proclamation "
that God is light from Christ? There are no words, spoken anywhere in the gospels by Jesus, in which this is directly said. The
answer to this question therefore is that we have this " proclamation " that God is light from Christ to the extent that Christ
revealed God as love. The connection between the proclamation
that " God is light " and the idea that " God is love " which
has now been made will be made clearer in the course of the
elucidation of the text. It is, however, possible to say now that
this connection between the two ideas may well be the key to
the whole letter. One proof that this supposition does in fact go
to the heart of the matter is to be found in 2 : 9–11, in which the
" darkness " is connected with hatred of one's brother and the
light with love of one's brother. Finally, it is important to point
out the view underlying these various statements, namely, that
the attitude of him who leads his life according to God is that
of love resulting in a total surrender of self, whereas the sinful

attitude is selfishness resulting in stubborn uncharitableness. ("Whoever looks at himself emits no light.")

Walking in the Light and in Darkness (*1 : 6—2 : 11*)

This section, with its two sub-divisions—the first exposition of the theme of " Christian and sin " and the first exposition of the theme of the commandment of love "—presents the exegete with special difficulties of its own. At first sight, the ideas contained in it seem to be hardly possible to set in order and even to be confusing and indistinct. In reality, however, the author has considered his ideas with extreme care. They are not developed each one from the preceding thought, in the way in which we are accustomed to reason, but progress antithetically in parallelisms. In addition, all these concepts are used here in rather a different sense from the one in which we use them today. The word "truth," for example, is a completely inadequate rendering of the corresponding Greek word *aletheia* used in the Johannine sense (see below). How, then, did the author come to employ these concepts and ideas in such a general and abstract way?

These concepts were not so unfamiliar to the people to whom the author was writing as they are to us today. They were current in the religious environment of gnosticism and late Judaism in which the author and his readers lived. Both of these movements, but especially the second—in the form of the theology of Qumran—must be considered if these religious and historical presuppositions are to be scientifically elaborated.

Thus we must, of course, make every attempt to understand, in the sense in which the author himself intended them to be understood, both the fundamentally general and abstract nature of his statements expressed in concepts which were determined by the period in which he was living and his specifically Christian insight, which often makes his statements in a special way concrete.

First Exposition of the Theme of "Christian and Sin" (1:6—2:2)

⁶If we say we have fellowship with him while we walk in darkness, we lie and do not live according to the truth; ⁷but if we walk in the light, as he is in the light, we have fellowship with one another, and the blood of Jesus his Son cleanses us from all sin. ⁸If we say we have no sin, we deceive ourselves, and the truth is not in us. ⁹If we confess our sins, he is faithful and just, and will forgive our sins and cleanse us from all unrighteousness. ¹⁰If we say we have not sinned, we make him a liar, and his word is not in us.

¹My little children, I am writing this to you so that you may not sin; but if anyone does sin, we have an advocate with the Father, Jesus Christ the righteous; ²and he is the expiation for our sins, not for ours only, but also for the sins of the whole world.

In the case of these three sentences beginning with "if we say," the author is clearly including in this "we," his fellow Christians. For he was of the opinion that the doctrines of the false teachers were a danger to Christians and it is not simply a question of a danger threatening the Church from outside, but the lives of Christians themselves which are at stake.

On the basis of a schematic breakdown of the structure of this section, it is important to note that the following contrasts can be found in verses 6 and 7: walking in darkness—walking in the light; alleged fellowship with God = lie = not living according to the truth—fellowship with one another.

The following contrasting pairs can be found in verses 8 (and 10) and 9: saying we have no sin—confessing our sins; we deceive ourselves (we make him a liar)—he is faithful and just; the truth is not in us (his word is not in us)—he will cleanse us from all unrighteousness (Jesus Christ is the expiation for our sins).

In verse 6, for the first time in the letter, we find a reference to a proud claim made by the false teachers—something which we shall encounter again—that they have fellowship with God. But their conduct proves that this is a lie—they " walk in darkness." What does the word " darkness " mean? Does the sinner walk in darkness because it is in the dark that evil deeds which will not bear the light of day take place? Or should we rather bear in mind what we said about 1:5 and interpret the word " darkness " as the repellent cold of uncharitableness and the blackness of hatred?

Not only the false teachers, however, have fallen victims to this danger. Christians are also faced with the danger of " lying " by " not living according to the truth." In the Johannine texts, " truth " is very different in meaning from " truth " in Hellenistic and especially in gnostic thought and far more akin to " truth " in the Old Testament, Jewish sense. In Semitic usage, truth was an action, something *done* (see, for example, John 3:21: " he who does what is true . . ."). The author of 1 John therefore regarded truth as an event or as a sphere of salvation taking place in action, as the divine reality revealing itself. " Not living according to the truth " or better, " not *doing* the truth," thus means not realizing the claim made by the divine reality in its self-revelation.

This " not doing the truth " is a " lie," not only in words (" if we say . . ."), but also in moral conduct (a " moral lie "). Basically, this " lying " is not simply a human failure. It is above all a lie directed against God. If a man says he has fellowship with God, yet walks in " darkness," he is to some extent saying, by virtue of this discrepancy between his assertion and his action, " God is darkness."

In verse 7 our author surprises us once again by using, as he did in verse 3 above, an unexpected phrase. If we walk in the light, we have, not an *imaginary* fellowship with God, but a real fellowship *with one another,* the concrete fellowship of brotherly love, in which true community or fellowship with God can express itself. And our being in this brotherly community of love is the prerequisite for our being cleansed by the blood of Jesus.

This saying, that we are cleansed by the blood of Jesus, strikes us today either as strange or as hackneyed, a mere cliché. How can we accept a statement such as this concerning the blood of Jesus in faith nowadays, and how can we possibly proclaim it as something to be believed? We can do this on one condition only. We have to ask and try to answer this question: What was meant by the author of 1 John—and by the New Testament as a whole—by " cleansing " or " purification by the blood of Jesus "? It is not enough to say that this is simply an expression of the primitive Christian idea of expiation and to point to the canticle of the suffering servant of Yahweh in Isaiah 53. We should certainly not be able to do very much with that today— from a fully justified fear of being misunderstood as stressing the " magical " element. Sins are not removed by the " blood " of Jesus as such, but by the love of God which is revealed in the self-surrender of Jesus, his only Son (see 1 John 4:9f.). Is this " blood " of Jesus therefore only a cipher for the love of God?

We must not overlook the fact that the text does not say: " the blood of Jesus has cleansed us " in the past, but " cleanses us " in the present. Apart from 1 John, too, there is another

New Testament text in which we read about purification by the blood of Jesus—the Epistle to the Hebrews. The author of this letter, moreover, had not only Jesus' crucifixion on Golgotha as a past event in history in mind, but also the risen, exalted Christ in heaven, interceding for us with the Father.

Whoever, despite his "walking in darkness"—his moral failure—claims to have fellowship with God (see under v. 6) may not have the slightest inkling that his conduct is sinful. The false teachers, the gnostics, were therefore probably convinced that they in fact had " no sin." The author of 1 John was, however, aware that this wrong attitude always constituted a real danger for Christians as well. The Christian who has so lost sight of the real God that he imagines himself, despite his sinfulness, to be assured of fellowship with God and of salvation and is no longer conscious of his sins " deceives himself." This is an increase or heightening of the " we lie " in verse 6. The " truth " cannot ultimately be in the man who in this way argues away his sins. As already indicated, " truth " in John means the divine reality in its self-revelation. If, then, the truth in this Johannine sense is not in a person, the divine reality is also not in him, so that he can have no fellowship with God.

The cure for self-deception, the reluctance to admit that we are sinful, is to " confess our sins." When we do this sincerely, God will prove his faithfulness and righteousness to us, in striking contrast to our self-deception, by forgiving our sins. This forgiveness of sins is salvation, contrasting with the situation without salvation in which man finds himself when " the truth is not in him." But how can we visualize this confession of sins in a really concrete manner?

1 John 1:9 does not refer directly to the sacrament of penance (which was, of course, not recognized in the early Church as a sacrament in the present dogmatic sense), but to the whole process of the confession of sins. What the author of 1 John, as a

Christian believer whose faith was rooted in Old Testament and later Jewish religiosity, meant by this " confession of sins " was not only penitential prayer in the secrecy of one's heart, but a confession which took place in the presence of other Christians, and almost certainly not exclusively in the presence of those holding office in the Christian community (cf. Jas. 5 : 16 : " Confess your sins to *one another* "). It is only in this way that the author's intention to do away with self-deception and to emphasize the importance of the community can be maintained. The contemporary form of confession of sins by receiving the sacrament of penance is also included in this passage. In the Church's recognition in the course of time of the fact that the forgiveness of sins constitutes a sacrament, we can perceive on the one hand the most concentrated realization of the content of this Johannine text. On the other hand, however, 1 John 1 : 9, together with James 5 : 16, can also be seen as a very powerful reason for not limiting the practice of confessing sins simply and solely to the reception of the sacrament of penance. Partly on the basis of these texts, this sacrament has come also to be seen within the framework of an extra-sacramental practice of penance—not only, therefore, in giving an account of one's personal actions to God and also not only in a liturgy of penance which is undoubtedly important in this context, but also and above all in spiritual dialogue between fellow Christians. The aim of this brotherly dialogue is especially to help other members of the community in their concrete situation with regard to God.

In verse 10 we find the last and most striking stage of the increase in the negative statements in our passage, the point where alleged fellowship with God and factual sinfulness ultimately part company : Whoever asserts that he has not sinned and does not have to bear the consequences of his sins makes God's word of guidance and forgiveness, the author says here, into the word of a liar. He completely does away with the concept of God expressed in 1:5, that God's light is incompatible with any trace of darkness. The "word," which has power to save and to establish a community, cannot be in a person of this kind. "His word is not in us" in verse 10 is the parallel statement to "the truth is not in us" in verse 8. By equating it with the "divine reality in its self-revelation," the author shows a very profound understanding of the "word."

Although it is clear that 1 John 2:1 marks a new beginning, it is also impossible to deny that, together with verse 2, it at the same time forms the conclusion to the preceding section. The sentence "I am writing this to you so that you may not sin" undoubtedly reads like the conclusion to the passage 1:6–10. What emerges on the one hand from this passage (1:6–10) is the conviction that Christians have to fight against sin (precisely because they have to "walk in the light") and, on the other hand, that the blood of Jesus cleanses them from that sin and from all unrighteousness (v. 7, see also v. 9). This thought is completed in 2:1f., in which it reaches its climax. One of the author's main aims certainly seems to have been to convey to his readers a joyful confidence that they would have fellowship with God. It is therefore quite possible that the idea might have arisen among these early Christians that there was no real need to fight against sin at all or at least to conduct this battle against sin very seriously, simply because the task of doing away with sins had been taken over by Jesus Christ. It is precisely to prevent this misunderstanding from arising, then, that the author includes this statement "I am writing this to you . . ."

Verses 1b–2 still form part of this conclusion, but not of the series of antithetic parallel statements (the contrasting "negative" and "positive" statements referred to earlier). The author did, however, still have in mind in these verses what he had already been talking about in the preceding verses, namely the need for Christians to acknowledge that they are sinners. He therefore took up the theme again in verse 1b–c: " But if anyone does sin . . ." It should be noted that he did not say, " But if anyone does sin, it is not very important "! This is, of course, far from what he believed. He was deeply convinced of the need to exhort Christians not to sin, but he was at the same time anxious not to stress this at the expense of Jesus' saving activity, which was, for him, of such paramount importance that it made any one-sided emphasis of the part played by man seem less urgent. The author of 1 John, believing as he did that man was cleansed by the blood of Jesus, could, after all, hardly have regarded man's sin as unimportant. But confidence in God's faithfulness and righteousness, the consequence of man's confession of his sins (see v. 9), would not be destroyed by man's sinning again—which was something that the author foresaw would happen.

Verse 2 says that Jesus is the " expiation " for our sins, or, more exactly, " atonement." This means the same as the statement in verse 7 that his blood cleanses us from all sin. What was said in verse 7 now becomes quite clear here in 2: 1f. In speaking of the " blood " or of the " atonement " of Jesus, the author did not only mean the past historical action of Jesus' crucifixion on Golgotha (although this was without doubt also included as the necessary foundation making all that followed possible). He was above all referring to the lasting significance of the glorified Jesus after his suffering and death. In other words, the author meant in verse 7 precisely what he meant later on in 2: 1, when he said " we have an advocate [paraclete] with the Father." He did not say that Jesus' saving act of dying on the cross was an " atonement." What he is in fact saying is that this atonement is brought about by the one who has died and who is now alive as our " advocate " (see Heb. 7 : 25). This means, in other words, that " atonement " is not something that Jesus has done—rather, it is Jesus himself in his person.

Jesus can be atonement for our sins as the one who has revealed the love of God for man in his death and who now lives, insofar as he is " righteous " and insofar as he is an " advocate." He is called, with emphasis, the " righteous " at the end of 2:1. " Righteousness " here does not refer to the virtue of one who gives what is his to everyone, but characterizes the one who has a right relationship with God and with his fellowmen. We read in 1 John 3:7 that " he who does right (=righteousness) is righteous, as he (=Christ) is righteous." The context tells us that this " doing righteousness " means the exercise of brotherly love as the characteristic of the man who is " born of God," the Christian. The prototype of this " righteousness," this acting rightly and having the right attitude in love, is Jesus Christ. His " righteousness " consisted in his committing himself totally during his life on earth for us (" he laid down his life for us," 1 Jn. 3:16) and thus revealing the love of God to us. This " righteousness " of love which gives itself totally is not something that happened only in the past. It is still living and takes away the sins of those who " know " him and who " abide in " him (see 3:5, 8). It pulls them away from the stranglehold of uncharitableness and hatred and gives them the strength to love. This " righteous " man, Jesus Christ, is, moreover, our " advocate " and " atonement." Fellowship with God, which cannot be attained without fellowship with the glorified Jesus, is what really achieves this atonement.

What, then, is the precise function of the basic idea contained in 2:1f. (and, of course, also in 1:7) with regard to the whole section which we have been considering (1:6—2:2), this passage in which the author is discussing the Christian's " walking in the light " and his " doing the truth "? It is, I believe, this. Christians do walk in the light, even though they also in fact sin.

But their " walking in the light " is made possible by the blood of Jesus and by Jesus himself as " atonement," in other words, by fellowship with the glorified Jesus Christ who is with the Father in an attitude of sacrificial love and total surrender.

FIRST EXPOSITION OF THE THEME OF THE "COMMANDMENT OF LOVE" (2:3–11)

A new theme is introduced in this section, despite the fact that the section does form a unity—and indeed a far closer unity than at first sight appears—with the preceding section. What first strikes us in the section we are to consider now is the author's use of new concepts. In verses 3–5, the key word " know " plays an important part—we " have known " or " know " him (God or Christ), but we " may be sure " (= " know " in the original Greek) that we " have known " or " know " him (v. 3) or that we " are in him " (v. 5). In verse 6, we encounter a typical Johannine concept: we " *abide* in him."

Furthermore, the main theme of the whole section (2 : 3–11) is stated at the beginning, in verse 3: " keep his commandments " (in the plural); " keep his word " in verse 5 (in the singular— " word " in the sense of " commandment "); " commandment " (in the singular) is also emphasized in verse 7f. In verse 6, " walk in the same way in which he [Christ] walked " is clearly an elucidation of the theme of " keeping his commandments." In verses 9–11, the leading concepts are " hating " and " loving," which are closely connected with the concepts " darkness " and " light," both of which are, of course, already familiar to us and both of which are also introduced earlier in this section, in verse 8. What we have to try to understand is the relationship between this " hating " and " loving " and the idea of " keeping the commandments " or the " commandment." Verse 5 would seem to indicate that there is in fact a connection between these concepts, because we are told there that the "love of God" is perfected in the man who keeps the word or the commandments.

We can therefore give the appropriate, although rather simplified heading of "commandment of love" to this section, which is the first of three in 1 John in which the author circles meditatively around this important theme and gradually illuminates it.

³*And by this we may be sure that we know him, if we keep his commandments.*

This sentence is obviously a transition to the new theme of "keeping the commandments." We know ("may be sure") "that we know him" by keeping "his" commandments ("his" being, according to what has gone before, Christ's and, of course, at the same time God's commandments). It should, incidentally, also be noted that this is the first occurrence in the letter of a series of statements, all of which similarly affirm how or in what way something definite can be "known." I have given the name of "knowing" formulas to these statements. This particular sentence (v. 3), moreover, certainly sounds as though reference had already previously been made to this "knowledge" of Christ or God and as though the readers of the letter urgently needed some norm by which to judge this "knowing." Yet, so far, nothing has in fact been written in the letter about this "knowing." Had it perhaps already been, in secret, a topic of discussion?

In the Johannine writings, as in the Old Testament, "knowing" is not only an intellectual process, but also something integral, a loving union. It is more or less what happens when one person "looks at" another person, instinctively knows him, and unites himself with him. Thus the word "know," in the Old Testament and even frequently in the New Testament, was also used to denote the most intimate union of man and woman in marriage.

"Knowing him" here in 1 John therefore means a most intimate relationship between man and Christ or God, fellowship with Christ and with God. What is more, for the author of the letter, Christ was so much one with God that fellowship with Christ was at the same time fellowship with God and that this was something which did not have to be said explicitly.

What the author in fact wants to say is therefore this: there is one norm for the one decisive factor that I have been speaking about and that is " keep his commandments."

He who says " I know him " but disobeys his commandments is a liar, and the truth is not in him.

"He who says . . ."—once again, as in 1:6, 8, 10 ("if we say . . ."), it would seem as though the author is referring to the false teachers. The presumptuous statement " I know him " has materially the same content as the statement made in 1:6—" If we say we have fellowship with him . . ." An extremely close parallel exists between this verse and 1:6.

Because it is impossible to " know " God without keeping his " commandments," the one to whom this verse refers is a " liar." The word " liar " had a much deeper meaning in the Johannine writings than it has in colloquial English today. It was the direct opposite of " truth " which, as we have seen, meant the divine reality in the act of revealing itself. " Lie " therefore denoted the act of building up a world of deception, an illusory reality, the " revelation " of evil, indeed of Satan, the adversary of God himself. Man, according to the writer of 1 John, was in the service of the evil one if he claimed to know God, yet refused to obey his and Christ's commandments.

⁵But whoever keeps his word, in him truly love for God is per-
fected. By this we may be sure that we are in him.

The positive content of this verse contrasts with the negative
content of the preceding verse 4. It is introduced by the phrase
" whoever keeps his word " (note that " word " is used here
instead of " commandment ") and this is followed at once by an
unexpected idea: " in him truly love for [of] God is perfected."
This is the first appearance in this letter, the great theme of
which is love, of this absolutely central concept. Two questions,
however, arise at once. First, what is meant here by " love for
God "? Is it our love for God, as the translation seems to suggest, or is it the love of God for us? Secondly, what is meant by
this love being " perfected " in us?

The fourth chapter of the letter contains a statement which
may help us to understand this verse. In 1 John 4:12, we read:
" If we love one another, God abides in us and his love is perfected in us." The whole context of this text in the fourth
chapter tells us that " his love " is the love which God showed
us in the total surrender of his Son, which he is himself in his
fullness as God and which he communicates to us so that it may
continue to be transmitted and to be effective in our love of our
brothers. A better rendering of this verse, then, would be " love
of God " or " God's love " is perfected in us.

This, however, brings us to our second question—how is God's
love perfected in us? It cannot simply mean, for example, that
his love is perfected in us insofar as all the possibilities of human
love are exploited in it. No, here too, the context both of 2:5
itself and of 4:12 provides the key to our understanding of this
" perfection " of love in us. According to 2:5, man, in whom
God's love, that is, the love that is derived from God, is perfected, knows that he is " in him," that is, in Christ or God.
In 4:12, too, this " perfected " love is closely connected with

fellowship with God (" God abides in us "). " Perfected " love, then, is the love which achieves, through this close link with God, a quality which lies beyond all human possibilities.

At the end of the verse, the author also introduces another new idea: " that we are in him." This too is an expression of man's fellowship with God.

In verse 5c, too, this idea of " being in him " as an expression of fellowship with God is connected with the theme of " knowing "—whoever keeps the commandments of God and Christ (whoever therefore loves his brothers) knows by this (the English text has " may be sure " here) that he is in God. Brotherly love, then, is the basis of our knowledge of our fellowship with God.

⁶He who says he abides in him ought to walk in the same way in which he [Christ] walked.

Like verse 4, this verse also begins with " he who says . . .", but here the author's aim is to make the consequences of the Christian's confession that he is " in Christ " quite clear to him, in other words, that he is obliged to walk, lead his life or conduct himself according to the example of Christ. But precisely what does this mean, " to conduct one's life like Christ "? Are there many different exemplary ways of behaving? No, there is only one and the author speaks of this one way of life in 1 John 3 : 16 when he says that Christ laid down his life for us, that he loved us to the end, to perfection. Anyone who says that he " abides in him," that he has " fellowship with Christ," must realize love as Christ realized it. This contains an echo of the typically Johannine version of the commandment of love: " This is my commandment, that you love one another *as I* have loved you " (Jn. 15 : 12).

⁷Beloved, I am writing you no new commandment, but an old

commandment which you had from the beginning; the old com-
mandment is the word which you have heard. [8]*Yet I am writing*
you a new commandment, which is true in him and in you,
because the darkness is passing away and the true light is already
shining.

The " commandments " are here reduced to the one " commandment." Even when the author of 1 John used the plural
form, " commandments," he really meant the one commandment
of love, since the individual commandments of God are no more
than the concrete expression of this one commandment applied
to different human situations and to different spheres of life.
The singular form " commandment " stresses the essential one-
ness of God's demand, as established in his one being and his
one revelation.

The commandment which the author is writing to tell his
readers of is both old and new at the same time. To what extent
is it " old "? The answer to this question will be found in
verse 7 itself. It is " old " insofar as Christians have had it
" from the beginning." This expression had two meanings,
closely interrelated, for the author of 1 John. In the first place,
" beginning " here means the beginning of man's life as a
Christian—his receiving faith and baptism. This " old " commandment is therefore part of the trustworthy and unchanging
Christian tradition. It is the commandment which the Christian
receives when he is baptized. In the second place, however,
" beginning " also has a deeper meaning—the meaning that it
has in the expression with which the letter itself opens in 1 : 1—
" from " or " since the beginning " or, according to the alterna-
tive translation, " since the origin," referring to the Logos of
life. We may therefore conclude that the author is also saying
here that this " old " commandment comes, like the one who has
given it (Christ himself), from the very beginning or origin of

divine life. In this sense, then, it is " old," simply because it is ultimately rooted in God's being, his love.

But in verse 8 this " old " commandment is also called " new." Is it because Jesus himself called his commandment a " new commandment " (Jn. 13:34)? Or is it rather because the author wished to emphasize the ever-new vitality of the Christian message as opposed to the new doctrines of the gnostics, who tried to diminish the value of the old teaching of the Christian community? Was the author of 1 John, then, perhaps saying this: the commandment that I am writing to tell you of is certainly old, but it is all the same newer than the doctrines of those who are opposed to the teaching of our community, in other words, it is a direct intrusion of the divine " newness of life " into our world? The author of the letter, however, himself provides the answer to our question as to why he is able to call this " old " commandment at the same time " new." It is, he says, because " the darkness is passing away and the true light is already shining."

The author, then, speaks of the " true light " in the immediate context of this exceptionally strongly emphasized commandment, the " word " which is to be kept (see 2:5). It is therefore extremely natural that we should be reminded here of the author's similarly very emphatic reference, in 1:5, to the " proclamation ": " This is the proclamation we have heard from him—Christ, the one who has existed since the beginning—that God is light."

But what is meant by God being always " light," yet only beginning to shine now? The statement made in 1:5 is not only about God's being, but also about his revelation—that he is certainly always " light," but that he has revealed himself only since a certain moment in time in such a way that the author of 1 John could say " the true light is shining." Since the appearance of the Logos of life, the " darkness " has been passing away

—the " true light," God himself as love, is revealed in Jesus Christ. That this is " new " means that it is filled with the vitality of the new light of divine love revealed in Christ, with the newness of the sacrificial love of Christ.

" Which is true in him and in you " or " and this is true in his case and in yours " means, on the one hand, that the existence of a " new " commandment here is true in his, Christ's, case, because Christ has revealed the love of God through the laying down of his life. It is, on the other hand, also true " in your case " (or " in you ") because, as far as you are concerned, the new light is already shining in your lives. In other words, the love of God and of Christ, which gives itself totally, is already visible and effective in your love of your brothers, in the power of God which enables you to love one another as brothers.

The dualism of " old " and " new " does not point to a tension between tradition and progress, then, but rather to quite a different tension. On the one hand, we have the trustworthy doctrine of baptism which is based on the eternity of the " Word." On the other hand, we have the " newness " of the norm of the love of Christ as a total surrender of self and of life itself and the everlasting " newness " of that love in contrast with the transient quality of the " world " and of " lust " (see 1 Jn. 2: 15–17). This commandment of love, then, is " old " insofar as it has its foundation in the life of God himself and is and has always been active in all his individual commandments. It is also " new " in that it has an absolute quality in the future. It is surely hardly possible for the absolute and universal significance of this commandment of love to be stressed more strongly than it is here by the author of 1 John.

⁹*He who says he is in the light and hates his brother is in the darkness still [so far].* ¹⁰*He who loves his brother abides in the light, and in it there is no cause for stumbling.* ¹¹*But he who*

hates his brother is in the darkness and walks in the darkness, and does not know where he is going, because the darkness has blinded his eyes.

The theme of light and darkness and the theme of the commandment and of love are closely bound together in these three verses. Verse 9 begins in exactly the same way as verse 4—and similarly to 1:6, 8, and 10—with the words " he who says . . ." All these statements refer to the wrong attitude held by the gnostics, something which at the same time constituted a danger for Christians. There is, however, an important difference in this passage (2:9-11). It is that the author's original intention is at last made unambiguously clear in these verses—that the darkness is hatred and the light is (divine) love. " Walking in the light " and " keeping the commandments " mean the same as loving one's brothers, whereas " walking in the darkness " is being held captive in hatred of one's brothers.

Verse 9 summarizes this explicit teaching in a negative form, stressing the darkness and hatred, and the two verses which follow, verses 10 and 11, amplify and elucidate this negative statement. Verse 10 states positively that the man who loves his brother is really in the light and that there is no need for him to " stumble." This means that he is borne up by the power of the light, the light that is God himself, and that he consequently abides in love and will not fall into the sin referred to in 3:4-10.

Verse 11 reiterates and clarifies the negative statement made in verse 9. A striking image is used to illustrate the disaster caused by hatred: the man who hates his brother loses all sense of direction, " because the darkness has blinded his eyes." In 1:8, the author wrote that the man who imagined that he was without sin was deceiving himself. Here we are told, with an almost unparalleled clarity, of the consequences of this self-deception, this " moral lie." Hatred of his brothers plunges man into total darkness. He becomes blind. He is seized and held captive by the " darkness," behind which a personal, evil power lurks.

A Twofold Conclusion (2 : 12–17)

THE GREAT ADDRESS: ASSURANCE OF SALVATION (2:12–14)

[12]*I am writing to you, little children, because your sins are forgiven for his sake. [13]I am writing to you, fathers, because you know him who is from the beginning [since the origin]. I am writing to you, young men, because you have overcome the evil one. [14]I write to you, children, because you know the Father. I write to you, fathers, because you know him who is from the beginning [since the origin]. I write to you, young men, because you are strong, and the word of God abides in you, and you have overcome the evil one.*

This sixfold address to Christians, the most impressive and the most solemn in the whole of the New Testament, follows here, apparently without motivation. In fact, however, it is in its proper place here.

What was said in 1:5—2:11 was so important for Christians that it had to define their understanding of themselves, in other words, what they thought about themselves in faith. What has been said so far in the letter is a message to Christians, a proclamation of what has happened to them, of what they now have access to, of what is now within their power. Everything that the author has said so far concerns them directly, and his purpose in this sixfold " great address " to Christians, these six sentences, is to impress this upon them. His aim is to impart to them a joyful awareness of what they are as Christians, a joy and confidence in their ultimate salvation. These six sentences, however, fulfill their function in the context in which they are placed only if they are translated: " I write to you that . . ."

At the end of the second and third parts of the letter, the author follows this same aim of arousing in his readers confidence in salvation, although he does it each time in a slightly different way. This was, after all, his principal intention in writing the letter. This can be seen very clearly in the first verse of the final section of the whole letter (5:13), where the writer says explicitly what he wants to achieve in the letter. The same purpose also applies to the section that we are considering now (2:12-14)—that Christians may know that they have " eternal life."

Two questions remain to be answered. The first is whether the author was not perhaps addressing different groups of people within the Church according to age, as it would appear at first sight from the text. If we examine the text more closely, however, we cannot fail to see that what he says to the " children " applies equally well to young men and women and to old people and that what he tells the " fathers " and the " young men " applies too to all Christians. This will become more apparent when we come to the individual analyses of the three addresses.

The second question concerns the change of tense which occurs in the original text, in which the past tense (" I have written to you ") is used instead of the present (" I am wording " or " I write ") in the second set of three addresses. This is generally accepted as a stylistic device employed for the sake of variety and is consequently not always observed in modern translations. On closer inspection, then, this sixfold address clearly consists of two closely related groups of three addresses.

The First Address. " I am writing to you, little children, because your sins are forgiven for his [Christ's] sake "—" because you know the Father." The readers are here addressed as

" children," a form which the author frequently uses. Are we to assume therefore that he looked on himself, with regard to his readers, as " father "? It is in fact occasionally clear that he does characterize the relationship between his readers and himself by the use of this form of address (" children "). An example of this is 1 John 2 : 1 : " My little children . . ."

What was his own view of his function as " father "? He supplies us with the answer himself in the " preface " to his letter. He saw himself as a " father " insofar as he was a witness of the eternal life made manifest in the flesh and insofar as he was the mediator of fellowship with God through fellowship with the witnesses, into whose company he draws his readers.

Our " great address," however, shows clearly that his attitude was in no sense paternalistic despite the fact that he was conscious of his function as " father." The address " children " in this case forms part of the message that our sins have been forgiven, which is, in all probability, an allusion to the author's words about the forgiveness of sins in 1 : 7, 9 and 2 : 1f., and also, beyond this, to baptism. " Children " here are Christians as baptized men and women who have fellowship with God by virtue of their faith and baptism.

Verse 12 could therefore be paraphrased to read : I am writing to you, baptized children of God (who are also my children, insofar as I am able to communicate to you fellowship with God as a witness of Christ).

The Second Address. " I am writing to you, fathers, because you know him who is from the beginning [since the origin]." This address occurs twice and, apart from the stylistic change of tense in the introductory verb, the wording is exactly the same in both versions. " He who is since the origin " is, of course, as in 1 : 1, Jesus Christ. This knowledge of Christ is in no sense something that is only applicable to Christians of greater age, since we read in verse 14 that knowledge of the Father, which always goes together with knowledge of Christ, is attributed to the author's " children "—a form of address used, as we have seen, for all baptized Christians.

The author has already discussed this knowledge of Christ with regard to all Christians in 2: 3ff. If we examine this repeated sentence in the light of what the author has said in 2: 3ff., the meaning becomes clearer. The author is saying, you know Christ because you keep his commandments—or you are not liars, like those who claim to have knowledge of Christ, but do not have it because of their sinfulness. Finally, later on in the letter, we find a statement which says that all Christians " know " (2: 20).

But why are the readers—ourselves—called " fathers " here? The answer is that we have joined the ranks of the *witnesses* because of our " knowledge of Christ," that is, our faith in Christ and the fellowship with Christ and the Father which this faith brings about. The author regarded those whom he addressed as " children " and to whom he was able to communicate fellowship with God at the same time as " fathers " who had joined him as witnesses. Is there any better way of overcoming any tendency to paternalism than the way followed here by the " elder " of 2 and 3 John?

The Third Address. The author here reaches a climax in his three addresses. The first address to the " young men " in verse 13b (" because you have overcome the evil one ") is included in its entirety in the second, complete version of this address (v. 14c), which consists of three parts.

But surely " being strong " and " overcoming " are above all characteristics of youth and of young men in particular. Does the author really want his words to be applied to all Christians in this case? Yet the second clause in verse 14c (" because the word of God abides in you ") can hardly refer to a special age group (see also 1: 10; 2: 5, 7). And what about " overcoming "? In other places in the letter, this word is certainly applied to

Christians as such, without regard to age—in 4:4, we read: "Little children . . . you have overcome them [the pseudo-prophets]"; in 5:4 it is very clearly stated: "For whatever is born of God overcomes the world; and this is the victory that overcomes the world, our faith"; and finally another clear reference in 5:5.

Anyone who listens with complete openness to this message will acknowledge the power that it contains. There is in fact hardly any other place in the New Testament where such a meaningful and concentrated message about our existence as Christians can be found.

WARNING AGAINST "LOVE OF THE WORLD" (2:15-17)

It is generally agreed that, for John, the "world" or *kosmos* was the sphere in which the personal power, hostile to God, the "ruler of this world" (Jn. 12:31) held sway. This power has, furthermore, already been named in the preceding verse of the letter (v. 14c). He is the "evil one."

The "world," then, which the author of 1 John tells us not to love, is, in this passage, neither God's material creation nor the personal world of human beings. It is rather the sphere of influence and activity formed within God's creation by this personal, evil power. We may go even further and say that this sphere of power formed by the evil one comes into contact and into conflict with the sphere of influence which proceeds from God and Christ. We can therefore say with confidence to modern Christians who are troubled by the Johannine teaching about the "world" that they should on no account place a low value on God's good creation or regard it as "filled with evil desires," but that they are bound to recognize that it is a sphere of conflict, a battlefield. The author of our letter knew that his readers were engaged in this battle and also that God gave them the strength and power to fight it. For this reason, he already attributed to them the triumphant power of " young men " to win the battle in the preceding verses.

¹⁵*Do not love the " world " or the things in the " world." If any one loves the " world," love for [of] the Father is not in him.*

The author of 1 John has already spoken about a " love " in verse 10 and contrasted this most sharply with hatred, using the image of light and darkness. If the same contrast between light and darkness is in fact also at work here in this passage, then once again our whole impression of it may be fundamentally changed!

The second half of verse 15, which speaks of the absence of the love of God, does certainly seem to point to the fact that what the author meant here by the " world " that we should not love was everything that proceeded from the sphere of influence and activity of the evil one or that was left in its wake, in other words, the " darkness " in exactly the same sense as this concept was used previously in 2:5-11, in contrast to " light." The second half of this verse says, in fact, that the love of the Father is not in the man who loves the " world " and the love of the Father is, as we have seen, the love which stems from the Father, that is, from the God who is " light " (see 1:5). This love, poured into us by the Father and coming from the Father (v. 16), leads us to walk in the light, that is, to love our brothers. Is the " world," then, the source and origin of all that is opposed to this love—cold uncharitableness and hatred of our brothers?

¹⁶*For all that is in the " world," the lust of the flesh and the lust of the eyes and the pride of life [in possessions], is not of the Father, but is of the " world."*

This threefold " worldly " desire is the breeding ground of uncharitableness and is radically opposed to " walking in the light." The third of these desires, " pride of life " or " pride of possessions," reveals this most clearly because it is the attitude of the man who possesses the world's goods already and closes his heart to his brother.

" Lust of the eyes " is also clearly diametrically opposed to love, whether it takes the form of a desire for possessions, a thirst for power, or a need to assert oneself over others. What the author means by " lust of the eyes " is obviously the need to possess and subdue everything and everyone he sees and who, like the man who is the victim of " pride of life," closes his heart selfishly to his brother.

What, then, can we say about " lust of the flesh"? First of all, we should not necessarily limit ourselves to the usual interpretation and think of this desire simply as a breaking of the sixth commandment. " Lust of the flesh " should rather, in accordance with the biblical concept of " flesh," be understood very generally here as the wrong direction taken by man's desire, stemming from his weakness as a creature or, beyond this, from his fallen nature. It is, in a very general sense, what impels him towards the darkness. In other words, it has to be seen as the concept which is superior to the other two. Moreover, as we have seen, the author has already shown us in his letter that " walking in the darkness," as the " sin " which is opposed to the commandment of Jesus to love, is incompatible with brotherly love.

" All that is in the world," then, is sinful egoism, opposed, in all its various forms, to the love that comes from God. All three expressions of " desire " refer ultimately to the same turning in on oneself, the same giving of oneself without reserve to the darkness which blinds one's eyes, the same absence of love seen from different points of view. This threefold desire which comes

" from the world " (that is, from the " evil one ") is the precise antithesis of what comes " from the Father," in other words, love which gives itself totally. This threefold desire is the fuel which sets light to hatred of one's brothers. The same conclusion can also be reached by using another image—that of man's experience of the cold, which is closely related to his experience of the darkness. This desire is, in this sense, what deprives love of its power and makes it grow cold.

What the author is requiring of his readers in these verses, then, is not a contempt of the world, a complete turning away from the world as such, but a renunciation of everything which makes love impossible.

¹⁷And the " world" passes away, and the lust of it; but he who does the will of God abides forever.

This verse provides a link with verses 12–14, in which the author, in his " great address " to Christians, assured them of their salvation. Here he says clearly that the " world," which, as we have seen, means the evil one's sphere of influence and activity, is not a lasting reality. It will " pass away " together with men's " worldliness " in the Johannine sense—their " lust," their desire for possessions and for power over others, their need to assert themselves and their turning inwards on themselves. This is contrasted sharply with the situation of those who do the will of God, like Jesus himself, who, according to the gospel of John, said: " I seek not my own will but the will of him who sent me " (Jn. 5:30). They abide forever with Jesus. This is the fulfillment of the " victory," the " overcoming " referred to in verses 13b and 14c.

The Second Part of the Letter
(2:18—3:24)

Because it is open to doubt whether the " preface " (1 : 1–4) and the section 2 : 12–17 really belong to the first part of the letter, the unity of this first part is not entirely unambiguous. The fact that the second part of 1 John (2 : 18—3 : 24) was composed as a single unit is, on the other hand, much more obvious.

The sequence of thought in the second half of this second part (3 : 4–24) is visible at once. Both in the formal sense and as far as the content is concerned, the second exposition of the theme of " Christian and sin " is linked in the clearest possible way by verse 10 to the second exposition of the theme of the " commandment of love." Similarly, the address to Christians, assuring them of their salvation, at the end of this part (3 : 19ff.) is also closely linked in its reasoning with the theme of the " commandment of love " by verses 18 and 19 and also by verse 14.

What is more, the second exposition of the theme of " faith in Christ " is also much more closely connected with the second exposition of the theme of " Christian and sin " than it would at first sight appear to be. This is achieved by the close involvement of the themes in the transitory passage 2 : 28—3 : 3, which is, in fact, far more than a mere transition.

Second Exposition of the Theme of "Faith in Christ" (2 : 18–27)

There is no obvious transition between the preceding passage and this section, which introduces two completely new elements. The opening words " It is the last hour " lead into a series of eschatological statements. These statements refer, in other words, to the end of time which is to be brought about by God and qualify the present time as the decisive period before the end.

The author at the same time directly links the false teachers who are endangering the faith of the community to which he is writing with these eschatological thoughts.

The structure of the section consists of three parts. The central part, a group of three verses (vv. 22–25), deals with the content and meaning of faith in Christ. This central part is preceded and followed by a group of verses (vv. 19–21, 26–27), in both of which Christians are contrasted with the false teachers who are trying to lead them astray. The real theme here is: How far can Christians judge these false teachers? These two groups of verses (vv. 19–21 and vv. 26–27) form, as it were, the framework enclosing the statements about the content and meaning of faith in verses 22–25. But they do more than this; they are also the key giving personal access to faith in Christ, the bridge between the individual Christian and the content and meaning of his faith in Christ or the door opening on to the mystery of individual faith. This framework of verses preceding and following the central group of verses on the content of faith thus corresponds to some extent to the address to the " fathers " in 2 : 13f.: " because you have known him who is from the beginning," that is, Christ. This section too can be understood in the light of this " aim " to convey the message of happy awareness of the knowledge of Christ and fellowship with God.

THE INTRODUCTION (2:18)

[18]*Children, it is the last hour; and as you have heard that anti-christ is coming, so now many antichrists have come; therefore we know that it is the last hour.*

This " last hour " is the time immediately before the end. The author is not attempting to predict the end precisely here. He is not trying in any way to indicate how long this " last hour " will last. All that he is saying is that this hour is the decisive period before the parousia of Christ and that it has come. The antichrist expected by Christians has been described in vivid apocalyptic terms (see 2 Thess. and Rev.). This idea of the antichrist was even changed by the author's statement that the antichrist was in fact already present in those who denied Christ.

Christian awareness of living in this " last hour " is therefore of great significance. Christians individually and the Church as a whole have an inescapable task to bear witness to and present in a thoroughly credible way the fact that the last hour has come.

The Contrast of False Teachers and Christians in 2:19–21

[19]*They went out from us, but they were not of us; for if they had been of us, they would have continued with us; but they went out, that it might be plain that they all are not of us.*

In this verse, we have the answer to a question, an urgent question, which troubles the author. How can it happen that these antichrists, these false teachers, can emerge from the ranks of the chosen members of the community of Christ? The answer is that they never, from the very beginning, really belonged to the Christian community—they were, to translate the text more literally and more exactly, " not out of us." This phrase, " not out of us," has a rather deeper meaning than " they did not belong to us " or, as the Revised Standard Version has it, " not of us." It means that they never lived from the same sphere of power represented by the word " us," in other words, the Christian community. Does this also mean, then, that these false teachers did not in fact decide of their own free will against Christ?

The question as to whether these false teachers were from the very beginning excluded from fellowship with God or were to some extent predestined to be " antichrists " does not really concern us here. The author recognizes that Christians had fellowship with God by the fact that they kept his command-ments. In just the same way, he saw that these men whom he called " antichrists " had never really lived from the same source of power as the Christian community by the fact that they denied Christ.

²⁰*But you have been anointed by the Holy One, and you all know.* ²¹*I write to you, not because you do not know the truth, but because you know it, and know that no " lie " [false teaching] is of the truth.*

Here the author states that what distinguishes the Christian from the " antichrist " is the source of knowledge which keeps them and strengthens them in their faith in Christ. The " anoint-ing " referred to here undoubtedly denotes the Holy Spirit, and the phrase " by the Holy One " means " by Christ."

But what does the author mean by this? We are led back to the idea expressed in the address to the " fathers " in 2:13f.: " you know him [Christ] who is from the beginning." But what does this idea mean in this context? It is clear from the emphasis given to it in verse 21 that it is important—in the second of this pair of verses, the author stresses that he wants to fill Christians with the confidence and firm conviction that they " know the truth " and that he wants to avoid any misunderstanding of his letter which might result in their thinking that he is writing to them to say that they did not know the truth (and therefore had to depend on purely human teachers). Christians know the truth and they also know that the opposite to the truth is the " lie," which does not come from the truth and cannot be reconciled with it. But is false teaching this " lie "?

It is advisable, however, to break off here and to content ourselves with this simple comment on the idea contained in this pair of verses. We can safely postpone any attempt to explain the basic meaning of these statements until we come to the second, much clearer expression of the same idea at the end of this passage, in verse 27. This pair of verses, verses 20 and 21, can be more easily understood in the light of this later statement.

The Contrast of False Teachers and Christians with Regard to the Content of Faith (2:22–25)

The most important aspect of these verses is that they make all salvation—the " eternal life " of verse 25—dependent on the Church's confession of Christ. It is possible to say that the author here unites the confession of Christ or Christology in the fundamental sense of the word with the confession of God or theology and fellowship with God.

Here, however, we are at once confronted with a question. Can man's salvation and fellowship with God be made exclusively dependent on orthodox teaching in this way? Or is the orthodox confession of God perhaps intended in a less one-sided and subtle sense, as our knowledge of the mistakes made in later religious controversies has taught us?

The difficulty becomes even greater when we read the author's characterization of the false teacher as the " liar " in verse 22:

²²*Who is the liar but he who denies that Jesus is the Christ? This is the antichrist, he who denies the Father and the Son.*

How is the man who denies that Jesus is the Messiah a liar—or even *the* liar? It is possible to understand that a man whose

life is not in accordance with what he claims is his fellowship
with God is a " liar " (1:6), but is it not possible for someone
who denies Christ simply to be in error? It is not very helpful
to recall that questions of this kind were not known or appreci-
ated at the end of the first century in the same way as they are
now. To do this would simply be to shift the emphasis of the
problem and even to miss the point of what is really being said
in the letter altogether. Although the author may perhaps not
have had our tolerant attitude towards those " in error," he may
nonetheless be saying something which applies to us as well.

We should not forget that the " antichrists " whom he is
attacking in the letter were not " heretics " of the kind encountered in later religious controversies. No, these liars or
" deceivers " (2 Jn. 7) were not in any sense Protestants or
Reformers; they were men who undermined the foundations
of faith in such a way that the whole structure of Christianity
was threatened with destruction. At every period of history,
including the present, Christians therefore have to ask this question—and this is where the author's message is relevant to us
as well—does the danger threaten the foundations of our faith
or not? What is more, because the dividing line between faith
and lack of faith also passes right through each one of us,
we must also ask ourselves this question.

The basic meaning of the Greek verb, usually translated here
by " to deny," is a clear indication of the fact that what we
have here is not simply an intellectual denial of or an inability
to understand dogma. This verb *arneisthai* means " saying no "
in the sense of refusing or rejecting a personal fellowship. Thus
this " denial " on the part of the false teachers is really a saying
no to the " Son," a refusal or rejection of fellowship with him.

It is, of course, clear from the context of verse 22 that *arneisthai*
is here used in the usual sense of our " deny," but this denial
or saying no to the truth that " Jesus is the Christ " (or Messiah)

is at the same time also a saying no to the Son and to the Father, which is, in other words, a refusal or rejection of fellowship with the Son and with the Father.

We may therefore possibly translate verse 22 as: Who is the liar but he who, saying no (refusing or rejecting fellowship), claims that Jesus is not the Messiah? Verse 22 also links this " denial " of the Son together with the " denial " of the Father. If we are to understand why saying no to the Son is at the same time also saying no to the Father, we must also think of other Johannine passages such as: " He who has seen me has seen the Father " (Jn. 14: [6], 9). The typical Johannine solution to the problem is to link together a powerful bond with Christ, a Christocentrism, with a radical biblical monotheism.

[23]No one who denies the Son has the Father. He who confesses the Son has the Father also.

In this verse, too, the purely intellectual sphere of " having " a correct or " orthodox " faith in the Father if we confess the Son is completely transcended. The meaning of this verb " to have " here is to have fellowship with and even more than this—if we confess the Son, we really have fellowship with God, we really *have* the Father of Jesus Christ *as our own father.*

[24]Let what you heard from the beginning abide in you. If what you heard from the beginning abides in you, then you will abide in the Son and in the Father. [25]And this is what he has promised us, eternal life.

The message of Christ is to " abide." An imperative is expressed here, so that the promise may result from it.

What is this " that was heard from the beginning " which is to abide in the Christian? Is it simply a confession of " orthodox " faith or is it perhaps connected (in some way which is not yet clear to us) with the " old commandment " of 2:7? This " old commandment " which Christians have " had from the beginning " consists, according to 2:7, of the word which they have heard. What we must above all bear in mind here is that the " abiding of the word " in the Christian which makes faith in Christ and fellowship with God possible is a much greater and more far-reaching reality than the simple acceptance of dogmas.

In verse 25, we are told explicitly that Christ's " promise " of " eternal life " consists of the fellowship with God and Christ that is to come, in other words, the fellowship that we shall have at the end of time. (This is clear from the use of the future in verse 24: " you will abide.") And Christ's promise is what our lives are directed towards.

THE CONTRAST OF FALSE TEACHERS AND CHRISTIANS ACCORDING TO 2:26–27

[26]*I write this to you about those who would deceive you;* [27]*but the anointing which you received from him abides in you, and you have no need that anyone should teach you; as his anointing teaches you about everything, and it is true, and is no lie, just as it has taught you, abide in him.*

These verses close the framework surrounding the central group of verses (vv. 22–25) on the content of faith, and Christians are once more contrasted with those who " deceive " them or lead them astray. The author again refers to the " anointing " that Christians have from Christ as the element which distinguishes them from the false teachers.

In this context, we should also note that, as the words " from

him " at the beginning of verse 27 refer to Christ, the word
" anointing " is also an allusion to Christ, the " anointed one."
We have the Holy Spirit as *our* anointing from him who was
originally anointed with the Holy Spirit and is therefore called
Christ, the " anointed one."

We are told here that this " anointing " that we have from
the " anointed one " " abides " in us. As we have seen, the
author uses the verb " abide " to denote a lasting state of con-
tinuing to be in someone.

The " anointing " of baptism had an effect on us when we
received it and it also " abides " in us. To express this more
acccurately, the spirit of Christ, who led us to faith and baptism,
" abides " or continues to be in us as a constant source of
strength which determines our lives.

All that the author has said so far about " anointing," however, reaches its climax in the statement that it " teaches " us
" about everything," so that we have no need for anyone to teach
us. What precisely does this mean? Does the author intend to
stress here the full spiritual authority of each individual Christian
at the expense of the authority of the Church's teaching office?
This is surely out of the question, if we recall the emphasis
placed at the beginning of the letter on the function of the
witnesses (1 : 1ff.). What the Spirit of Christ teaches Christians
about is materially exactly the same as what they have " heard
from the beginning " (v. 24). And what, then, is that?

The answer to this question can be found in the gospel of
John—in John 14 : 26, in 15 : 26f. (the Paraclete and, in his power,
the disciples, bearing witness), and above all in 6 : 44f.: " No
one can come to me unless the Father who sent me draws him
. . . It is written in the prophets, ' And they shall all be taught
by God.' Everyone who has heard and learned from the Father
comes to me."

A further question that we may ask is : Has this confession

of Christ anything to do with " walking in the truth "? In other words, is it concerned not only with faith, but also with love?

The whole passage, 2: 18–27, is, because of the references to " anointing " contained in it, in fact an elucidation of the address to Christians as " fathers " in 2: 13f., those who have known Christ as the one " who is since the origin [from the beginning]." It is, moreover, an application of this address to the concrete situation in which Christians were placed by the activity of the false teachers at the time the letter was written. We may therefore conclude that this passage also contributes to the author's aim of strengthening his Christians in their joyful confidence in ultimate salvation.

At the end of verse 27, we read: " just as it [the anointing] has taught you, abide in him." (It should be pointed out here that the pronoun in the last phrase undoubtedly refers to the anointing, so that a stricter translation would read " abide in it.") This promise of salvation of which the author is assuring his Christians cannot, however, be given by a witness of Jesus Christ unless he at the same time expresses the imperative " abide in it." The two—a promise of salvation and a call to the subject to prove his worth—are inseparable. Unless the Christian " walks in the light " as he is exhorted to do here, the promise of salvation becomes invalid. The opposite is also true: unless the Christian is assured of salvation, as he is here, he may keep the commandments, but his way of life will only be a pale reflection of the Christian life envisaged by the author of 1 John.

Expectation of Salvation, the State of Being Children of God, and the Christian's Moral Obligation (2 : 28—3 : 3)

This section is intended to connect the two (or three) major sections of this second part of the letter, which share a common train of thought, together, because the section containing the second exposition of the theme of " faith in Christ " (2 : 18–27) on the one hand and the two connected sections, " Christian and sin " (3 : 4–10) and the " commandment of love " (3 : 11–24) on the other are fundamentally no more than negative and positive variations on the same theme of the " commandment of love."

Looked at from the point of view of its thought, then, the whole section, 2 : 28—3 : 3, is a kind of intermediate link. It is, however, far more than just this. The question is, to what extent is it more than simply a linking passage?

The author bridges the gap between the two connected sections in the second part of his letter in the following ways. (a) He introduces the new minor theme of " being born of God " or of being children of God (which in fact continue the ideas contained in the previously introduced themes of fellowship with God and of knowing God). (b) He takes the eschatological theme of the preceding section, 2 : 18–27, to its climax in connection with this new theme. (c) Finally, he also connects the " imperative " theme of the call to Christians with the other two themes by interlacing these two themes and thus consolidates it.

This consolidation of the theme of the call to Christians is particularly important for the ideas included in the following passage. If we compare this following passage, 3 : 4–24, with the preceding section, 2 : 18–27, it becomes clear that the theme of the call to Christians which was contained in 2 : 24 and above all at the conclusion of this preceding section in verse 27 (" abide in it ") is continued in the following passage, 3 : 4–24, on a much broader basis.

In our present section, 2 : 28—3 : 3, however, we have much more than simply an artistic interlacing of three themes. This section is above all characterized by a stronger emphasis being placed on the " eschatological " theme, the theme of the expectation of salvation, than anywhere else in the letters or the gospel

of John. In this respect, the present section undoubtedly repre-
sents a climax in the Johannine writings.

*28And now, little children, abide in him, so that when he appears
we may have confidence [openness] and not shrink from him
in shame at his coming [parousia].*

This is the only time that the word parousia is used in the
Johannine writings. The call to " abide in him " is reinforced
by the reference to the coming of the Lord in judgment, something that was expected at that time by the whole Christian
community. The purpose of this verse is to ensure that Christians
should not be put to shame in his presence on the day of judgment and that they may have " openness," a word of which
early Christians were especially fond. What, then, is to happen
to those who " abide " in Christ at his judgment? It is not
simply that they will be spared. It is much more than this.
They will be saved. They will have freedom and joyful confidence in his and his Father's presence and this is the beatific
fellowship of the end of time.

*29If you know that he is righteous, you may be sure that everyone
who does right is born of him.*

The important new element in this verse is the phrase at the
end, " he is born of him [of God]." It is well worthwhile reflect-
ing carefully about uncommon phrases used for matters which
occur frequently in the New Testament. It is possible, after all,
that this phrase " born of God " may tell us more about our
relationship with God than the rather hackneyed " child of
God." But how did the author come to use this expression?
It is easy enough to see that he needs it for what follows and is

therefore using it here to lead up to the next step, but what does it mean within the sentence itself?

When the author says: " you may be sure . . ." or, to translate this phrase more literally, when he calls upon us to " know that . . ." his purpose is to go farther along the way towards the goal at which he was previously aiming—to tell us how we can gain confidence in salvation, or rather, to impress even more deeply on us that God makes it possible for us to have this great confidence and indeed gives it to us. We are not simply to have this " openness," this joyful confidence, for the first time on the day of judgment. On the contrary, we are to let it begin to germinate and grow more and more inside us even *now,* so that it provides us with the power to live as Christians here and now.

Quite clearly, Christ was meant in verse 28, whereas in verse 29 the expression " born of him " can only refer to God. Does the subject of the statement change, then? Is the thought in verse 29 new? Not at all. Verse 29 belongs closely to the whole thought of the section. Or has a source been exploited and is the joint still perceptible here? Even this is not likely. The apparent change in the subject can only be explained in the light of the particularly Johannine manner of seeing God and Christ in each other (see also above, 2: 22-25). Presumably, it is still Christ who is meant in the first half of verse 29, so that the sentence could be paraphrased as: If you know that he [Christ] is righteous (and thus proves himself to be God's Son), you may be sure that everyone who does right is born of God.

If this interpretation is correct, it certainly reveals, behind the apparent obscurity of the Johannine expression, a very deep significance in " being born of God." In other words, " being born of God " can only be understood fully in the light of Christ —the Christian can only become a " child of God " by sharing in the sonship of the one who is, by his very being, the " Son."

¹See what love the Father has given us, that we should be called children of God; and so we are. The reason why the " world" does not know us is that it did not know him.

In this verse, the author pauses to consider the thought that we are " born of God," although here he calls it being " children of God." There can surely be very few Christian concepts which have been made as meaningless by misunderstanding or as harmless by misuse and falsification as this expression. It is therefore absolutely necessary to try to approach it anew and to grasp its true dimensions. No doubt the author himself had to combat a pagan misunderstanding, a gnostic falsification, of the same concept.

In the Johannine sense, being " born of God " and a " child of God " is not something that applies to all men as God's creatures. It is rather an absolutely free gift, something beyond man's expectations and understanding. What is meant here by " child of God " is perhaps most clearly expressed in the prologue to the fourth gospel: " To all who received him, . . . he gave power to become children of God " (Jn. 1:12). To become a " child of God," it is necessary to have a " power " which no man has of himself and which only the Logos, the Son, can give. It is revealing that, unlike Paul, our author never calls Christians " sons " of God, but reserves the word " son " for Christ alone. But, although he uses different means from Paul's, he uses the same degree of emphasis to show that the unique sonship of Christ is the prerequisite for our being " children of God." The author of 1 John insists that we can be " children of God " or " born of God " only by sharing in the sonship of the one Son. If we " abide in him " and indeed because we " abide in him," we are not only *called* " children of God "—*we are so*. These few words added at the end of the verse—" and so we are "— are a more urgent call to reflect about the gift that has been bestowed on us than a long exposition of the theme " children of God."

The author, however, is anxious to draw our attention not only to our being " children of God " because of God's gift to us, but also and above all to the one who bestows this gift on us. " See what love . . ."—behind these restrained words, we detect a note of intense longing on the part of the author to lead us on to reflection about the love which bears us up and we know that this reflection can only be an expression of gratitude for God's gift.

²*Beloved, we are God's children now; it does not yet appear what we shall be, but we know that when he [or, " it "] appears we shall be like him, for we shall see him as he is.*

The theme of the expectation of salvation is brought to its climax in this verse. We would still be unaware of the real greatness of the gift that has been bestowed on us if it were not revealed to us as an infinite greatness. Being " born of God " and " children of God " has consequences which are as yet beyond our vision and this means that another and unsuspected transformation lies ahead of us.

It is absolutely essential for the Christian to know in the depths of his being that the ultimate reality is not yet present. There are more passages in Paul's writings than in John's in which this conviction is expressed, but our text, 1 John 3:2, leaves nothing to be desired as far as clarity is concerned.

It is worthwhile pausing here to consider the different ways in which Paul and John express this knowledge that the ultimate reality is not yet with us. Paul tends to use the category of creation. For him, eschatological fulfillment is " new creation," a new creation consisting of the resurrection from the dead, a resurrection to glory in participation of Christ's risen glory. (According to Rom. 8:23, we are still waiting to be " set up as sons.") John, on the other hand, is more inclined to use the category of revelation. In his view, eschatological fulfillment no longer consists of faith, which is awakened by revelation here on earth, but of seeing, which is our reaction to the ultimate, fulfilled revelation. Paul also uses the image of seeing, for example, seeing dimly in a mirror and, at the end of time, face to face in 1 Cor. 13 : 12, but the predominant idea in his case is that of creation.

No misunderstanding is buried so deep in modern Christian consciousness and does so much harm to Christian hope as the view that eschatological fulfillment, coming to rest in glory, will be tedious and dull compared with the passionate commitment that characterizes our lives here and now and can make them so precious!

³*And everyone who thus hopes in him purifies himself as he is pure.*

Once again the author returns to " calling " on his readers to consider their lives in the concrete. The strongest reason for " purifying " or sanctifying ourselves, that is, for abiding in Christ, is this Christian " hope " of eschatological fulfillment. In other words, the Christian will sanctify himself when he sees his being a " child of God " in the full dimensions revealed by hope of " that which has not yet appeared." This " hope " is hope of the greatness of the God who is light and love, since our ultimate fulfillment—what we hope for—is not devised by us, but by God. This hope can therefore and must strengthen and stimulate us in our Christian way of life, our " walking in the same way as Christ walked " (2 : 6). The Christian who has this hope is making himself holy by resembling, as far as it is possible for him to do so, the " pure " and " righteous " one, Christ himself, in other words, by " keeping his commandments " (2:3) so that Christ's way of life is the norm for his own conduct.

Second Exposition of the Theme of "Christian and Sin" (3 : 4–10)

The link between the new section of the letter and the previous one is formed by 3:3–4, both verses of which are similar in form and in structure: "Everyone who thus hopes . . . purifies himself "–" everyone who commits sin is guilty of lawlessness."

Two themes from the previous passage dominate this section. The first of these is the theme of " being born of God," and here it occurs especially in the form in which it is found in 2:29, where it is concerned with how being born of God can be known. The second is the theme of the call to " abide in him " (Christ). This call is based on the promise that his " anointing " abides in us. It is at the same time a call to " sanctification " and to " do righteousness."

Fellowship with Christ and "Sin" (3:4–8)

The three verses 3:4, 5 and 6 contain the principal statements made in this subdivision, one in each verse. Verse 4 refers to sin, verse 5 to Christ and his work against sin, and verse 6 contains, in both positive and negative forms, the central affirmation that the Christian, that is, the one who abides in Christ, does not sin. These three ideas are varied and developed in the two verses that follow, 7 and 8. In this way, the contrasting structure of the section and its sequence of ideas, expressed in opposing statements, are made quite clear.

Let us now take verses 4–6 as our guideline in our exposition of the section, at the same time making use of the statements in verses 7 and 8 which amplify and develop these ideas.

*Everyone who commits sin is guilty of lawlessness; sin is
lawlessness.*

At first sight, this statement seems strange and superfluous.
But the concept of " evil," translated here literally as " lawlessness," must have had a very definite meaning for those who
read this letter. For them, " evil " must have formed a clearer
contrast to "holiness " (" purification from sins," 3:3) than
" sin." In fact, the word " evil " or " lawlessness " *(anomia)*
must have been very familiar to the original readers of 1 John
from the descriptions of the eschatological period of disaster
before the end of the world which were current at the time.
In that context, the word referred to Satan's battle and his
power used against God and the chosen people of God. Clearly,
what the author is saying here is this: the " sin " that I am
referring to here is the evil of Satan directed against God, as
prophesied for the " last hour " in which we are living now
(2:18). We are obviously on the right track in this interpretation,
because verse 8 says in fact: " He who commits sin is of the
devil " and at the end of verse 8 sins are called the " works of
the devil."

What kind of sins or what kind of sin—the singular is used
in verses 4 and 8, where " sin " is clearly contrasted with
"justice "—can be characterized in this way? Has this word
" sin " a sound here, perhaps, which has not been heard before
in it? In 1:8f., we read of sins which Christians have to confess
and the Christians who confess these sins do not walk in darkness, but in the light (see 1:7). In the section 1:6—2:11,
however, this " walking in darkness " is discussed and we
recognized this to be in sharp contrast with brotherly love—
hatred (2:9f.). Is this darkness, in the narrowest and strictest
sense of the word, also being discussed here in 3:4ff., perhaps?
In any case, the full extent of evil, which was outlined in 1:5—

2:11 by the concept of "darkness," is characterized here—even more strongly than in 2:13–17—by the personal evil power.

⁵You know that he appeared to take away sins, and in him there is no sin.

Christ is the opposite to "sin" ("in him there is no 'sin'") and he is "righteous" (v. 7). This absolute opposite also had its effect in the purpose of Christ's appearance. He appeared in order to take away sins, in other words, to destroy the "works of the devil" (v. 8b).

This is, of course, the negative version of the "purpose" of Christ's appearance, but 1 John certainly contains more positive versions of Christ's purpose. In 4:14, for example, we read that the Father sent the Son as the "saviour of the world" and it is clear from the context that the Son's mission is to *reveal the Father's love.*

⁶No one who abides in him sins; no one who sins has either seen him or known him.

This is, of course, the first of the two central statements occurring in this section. The question as to what is precisely meant by this "sin" which the one who abides in Christ does not commit is raised most urgently here and in verse 9. We should certainly be misunderstanding the sense of both of these statements if we were to think of the word "sin" as meaning the same as it does today, that is, as everything that is contrary to any of the commandments, and if we were consequently to dilute the statement. By this, I mean that we should on no account think that the author did not really want to tell us that the Christian does not sin. We should not believe, for example, that he is simply expressing a demand to avoid sin with exceptional pungency or that what he is saying could only have been possible in a utopian period of Christianity (which has surely never existed). The author means exactly what he says.

We must accept these sentences just as they are in the text. As such, they are astonishingly absolute—anyone who abides in Christ (and does this not mean every Christian?) does not sin, in the sense in which it is understood here. We may be sure that the author cannot simply be saying what is obvious and indeed banal—that the man who keeps all the commandments cannot at the same time sin against those commandments.

The second half of this statement about the Christian's " sinlessness " is equally astonishing and problematical. The man who has neither seen Christ nor known him. This surely means that he has neither faith in Christ nor " knowing " love of him. But is it not a datum of human experience that it is possible for sin and faith in Christ and even love of Christ to exist side by side in one and the same person? The author undoubtedly accepts this himself in 1 : 8f. Or is Augustine right in his view —a view that is, incidentally, hardly held at all by modern exegetes or if it is, is put forward less consistently—that what is meant here is *sin against love*?

The best course that we can take here is to consider the intention of the letter as a whole, because it is only in the light of this total intention that we shall be able to see the author's intention in this passage. What the author is proclaiming to his readers is that their sins are remitted and that they have knowledge of God (this means fellowship with God) and a triumphant power, that they have in fact, through the power of God, already triumphed over evil. The aim of 1 John is to arouse a happy certainty of salvation in those who read the letter and to strengthen their joy and confidence in the grace of God which has already been given to them (and which is fully compatible with their constant struggle against sin).

"Being Born of God" and "Sin" (3: 9–10)

*⁹No one born of God commits sin; for God's nature ["seed"]
abides in him, and he cannot sin because he is born of God.*

The author here connects the idea of verse 6 with the theme of
" being born of God " and expresses it in an almost shocking
way, going so far as to say that the " child of God " *cannot* sin.
How is it possible for the author to intensify this idea to such
an extent? In the second half of this verse, what is apparently
the same justification is given—" because he is born of God."
In the first half, however, a new idea with apparently the same
meaning is placed parallel to this—" for God's seed abides in
him." The fact that the " seed " of God is the Holy Spirit in this
verse is suggested by the similar construction of the parallel
verse 2 : 27. In both cases, the " anointing " or the " seed "
abides in the Christian. Precisely the same applies in the case
of two other parallels in which the Spirit of God is explicitly
mentioned—3 : 24 and 4 : 13. According to these two parallel
verses, we know that we abide in God and that he abides in us
because he has given us of his own Spirit.

This statement about the Spirit as the " seed " of God helps
us to understand better the fact that we are " born of God," or
rather it takes us more deeply into the heart of the mystery
that is being proclaimed here. The word " seed " is, of course,
fully part of the whole terminology of procreation and birth.
The " seed " through which God begets his children—in this
case by giving them faith and baptism—is his Spirit. Any
possibility that the author's idea might be compared with the
biological process of procreation and that a misunderstanding
might in this way arise is, however, excluded by the statement
that this " seed " *abides.* After all, if what the author had in
mind was a natural pouring out or emanation of the divine

being, this seed which flowed from God would *become* the child of God. But it is clear from the text that this seed abides; it remains what it is, the Spirit of God himself. There is no mingling with matter here, as the gnostics living at the time that the letter was written and later gnostics assumed. It is only because of this that the author could call on Christians to " abide in him " and that the man who was " born of God " had to prove himself in his way of life or " walking."

The texts which parallel 3:9 take us even further. This is especially true of 4:13: " By this we know that we abide in him and he in us, because he has given us of his own Spirit." This statement is placed between two great statements about God occurring in the fourth chapter of the letter, " God is love." The more deeply we allow the words of this fourth chapter to penetrate into our minds, the more clearly we shall recognize that this is the mysterious center of the whole letter. The conviction that God is love is concealed within almost everything that is said in the entire letter.

As soon as we become aware of the extent to which this central affirmation that " God is love " is present in 3:4 and 3:10, for example, we can further our understanding of the passage by substituting the word " love " for " God," " he," or " him," remembering, of course, that " love " here can only mean the *personal* love which God himself is. In doing this, we are only doing what the author himself did, for example, in 4:8, 12, 16.

Thus paraphrased, 3:9 would then read: Whoever is born of love (which God himself is) does not sin, that is, he does not fight against this love, because the Spirit of God, as the seed of love which has made him the child of love, abides in him. Indeed, he cannot sin (with the diabolical sin of hatred, of denying love), because he is born of divine love. The " sin " referred to here is clearly and almost automatically recognizable in this exposition as the denial of divine love. It is not an abstract action against some divine commandment, but the concrete denial of God himself in his revelation. The opposite to " sin," then, is not simply " justice," but *love,* the love which comes from God.

[10]*By this it may be seen who are the children of God, and who are the children of the devil: whoever does not do right is not of God, nor he who does not love his brother.*

The final confirmation of this interpretation is found in verse 10, which shows clearly that the question at issue here is that of the " certainty of salvation." It is evident from verse 10a (" By this it may be seen who are the children of God, and who are the children of the devil ") that what we have here is the answer to our question, how do we know our salvation, our eternal life?

Our interpretation of 3:6, 9 is, however, more properly to be found in the second half of verse 10: " Whoever does not do right is not of God, nor he who does not love his brother." But verse 7 can also be regarded as providing an answer to this question as to how we can have joy and confidence that we shall be saved. The call, which makes us take notice—" Little children, let no one deceive you!"—points, like the statement in verse 10a about the making known of the children of God and the children of Satan, to the existence of the criterion by which salvation and its absence can be known. According to verse 10a and what has gone before, the children of the devil can be known by the fact that they sin and the children of God can be known by the fact that they do not sin, that is, against love.

Quite a large number of additional texts which confirm this interpretation can be found in 1 John. Some of these can only be seen as confirmations after long study, but others bear out our interpretation of 3:6, 9 fairly obviously. An example is:

" He who loves is born of God, and knows God " (4 : 7; see also especially 4 : 8a).

Second Exposition of the Theme of the "Commandment of Love"
(3 :11–24)

This section, like all the others which follow, also serves the author's intention to strengthen his fellow Christians' joy and confidence in salvation. Indeed, what was said on this subject in 3 : 4–10 is carried to its logical conclusion here and placed on a firm foundation.

THE PROCLAMATION "THAT WE SHOULD LOVE ONE ANOTHER" (3 : 11)

"For this is the message which you have heard from the begin-
ning, that we should love one another, . . .

Obviously, the author regarded the content of 3 : 11 as a message which was as triumphantly joyful as the proclamation made in 1 : 5. And indeed it is exactly the same message. The author could simply have repeated in 3 : 11 what he had already said in 1 : 5 and in fact he does repeat the sense of this earlier verse and at the same time clarifies it and takes it to its logical conclusion.

The relationship between the proclamation made in 1 : 5 and that in 3 : 11 is like the relationship between an indicative statement and the imperative that results from it. 1 : 5 is an indicative which is followed by this imperative of 3 : 11. The commandment of love can therefore be characterized, in 3 : 11, as a " proclamation " because the message of divine love is seen here in the light of its imperative character.

The proclamation " that we should love one another " is the same as the proclamation " that God is light " (1:5), because this version of the message also contains an imperative, namely, to " walk in the light " (1:6ff.), in other words, to love the brothers (2:9–11). In exactly the same way, the version of 3:11, the imperative construction, presupposes the indicative (or the content of faith) that " God is light " (and therefore love). This imperative version, in other words, includes the author's indicative statement. The " moral " or imperative message and the " dogmatic " or indicative message thus coincide. They are no more than two different aspects of one and the same proclamation.

The Dark Counterpart to Brotherly Love: Hatred as Murder (3:12–15)

[12]. . . *and not be like Cain who was of the evil one and murdered his brother. And why did he murder him? Because his own deeds were evil and his brother's righteous* . . . [15]*Anyone who hates his brother is a murderer, and you know that no murderer has eternal life abiding in him.*

This section falls into three parts. The first and the third parts (the negative counterpart to brotherly love) enframe the second, central part, which is addressed directly to Christians and refers to the antithesis between them and the " world " and especially to their confidence in salvation.

The Christian's attitude and behavior should be diametrically opposed to that of the first murderer Cain. He was " of the evil one," in other words, he was, in the sense of verse 10, a " child of the devil." He based his life on the law of God's adversary and " murdered his brother." The author has clearly decided to show what he meant by " sin " in 3:4–10 by giving

the example of the first murder in human history, that committed by Cain. He himself also asks the question, why did Cain
murder his brother?

But how can the fact that Cain's actions were evil and those
of his brother were righteous be a reason for Cain's murder of
his brother? Is it anywhere presupposed in the text that Cain
was, for example, envious of his brother's righteousness or of
the fact that God had approved of and accepted his brother's
sacrifice? No, the reason that the author had in mind goes
deeper. The murder was not, in the author's view, committed
out of envy, but out of the complete opposite to love—out of
hatred. The attitudes of Cain and of his brother Abel illustrate
clearly who belongs to the realm of light and who belongs to the
realm of darkness. The author " recognized in Cain's attitude
the primordial hatred of the man who was conditioned by darkness for the man whose behavior was determined by light."

We must now omit the next two verses, or most of their content, and go straight on to consider the third part of this section,
verse 15. This is because we can only really learn what verse 12
means for us today from verse 15. In itself, verse 12 might lead to
a Pharisaical attitude on the part of the Christian, who might be
persuaded to think that he is in no danger of falling into the
sin of Cain. But verse 15 shows clearly how verse 12 can apply
fully to any Christian. The last sentence (v. 14c) in the "en-
framed " central part of verses 13–14 provides a key to our understanding of the sin referred to in chapter 3. If all that was meant
was murder in the literal sense of the word—and this might be
the case if only verse 12 were taken into consideration—a
normally " decent " Christian would certainly be tempted to
think " this does not concern me." But any such Pharisaical attitude is at once made impossible by an examination of verses 14c
and 15. According to verse 14c, the absence of love is equated
with hatred. This is because the man who abides in the realm

of death, in other words, in the realm of darkness or the kingdom of the evil one, Satan, is characterized here, in parallel to
the man who "hates" in verses 13 and 15, as the one who
"does not love." It is, of course, possible to think of "not loving" and "hating" as differing from each other in kind or at
least in degree. If this view is correct, the author was therefore
only able to use the two terms interchangeably because there was
no difference in degree, for him, between not loving and hating.
But this is still minimizing what he wanted to say; he was
above all concerned with the need to characterize what is meant
by belonging to the realm of death and the condition of "sin"
which imprisons a man in the realm of death and is fulfilled by
the very fact of "not loving." The author's aim here is to suggest
quite forcibly that "not loving" is not in any sense unimportant, but that it is, on the contrary, in not loving that the
Christian falls away completely.

[13]*Do not wonder, brethren, that the " world " hates you.* [14]*We
know that we have passed out of death into life, because we love
the brethren.*

What is surprising is that the author does not warn his Christian
readers against the absence of love and hatred here in the central
part of the section, but once again strengthens them in their
joyful assurance of salvation. He does this, however, with the
hatred of the " world " in the background. One has the definite
impression that his intention here is to comfort his readers less
because they feel themselves to be weak than because they are
conscious of the harsh contrast between themselves and the
" world " and of the hatred of the " world."
    Just as Abel was hated by Cain, who was of the evil one,
because of his " righteous " actions, so too are Christians placed
in a harsh contrasting situation with the " world," which is

also of the evil one. They should not be surprised by this hatred, however, because it is accepted as a matter of course in 1 John that the light is hated by the darkness and consequently that those who love in the power of God are hated by those who deny love.

The love which causes Christians to be hated by the " world " must have been, for the author of 1 John, an attitude which was identical with the imitation of Christ, with being a disciple of Jesus. It must have been, for him, such a radical love, a love that was so alien to the " world," that the disciples of Jesus were hated because of it. They were hated because they did not base their love of their fellow men on the standards of this world, but linked it inseparably with Jesus' crucifixion and the shame and humiliation of the cross and with the call to follow their cruci-fied master and his example of love which gives itself totally. But—and this must make believers examine their consciences carefully—the " world's " hatred of Christians is only from the devil if it is directed against the message and the reality of the love of total self-surrender of the cross and not if it affects them because they are themselves going contrary to the message of Christian love.

BROTHERLY LOVE AS THE LAYING DOWN OF ONE'S LIFE (3:16–18)

[16]*By this we know love, that he laid down his life for us; and we ought to [are obliged to] lay down our lives for the brethren.* [17]*But if anyone has the world's goods and sees his brother in need, yet closes his heart against him, how does God's love abide in him?* [18]*Little children, let us not love in word or speech [alone] but in deed and in truth.*

In verse 14, we were concerned with the knowledge of salvation and our means of knowing this salvation was love. Here, we go a stage further and are concerned with the knowledge of love itself, the love of God and our love. The commandment of love is given a Christological basis here. The author first speaks of Christ's act of love, in which the love of God is made manifest. He cannot, however, speak of this without showing its consequences for us, that is, without speaking of the commandment of love. We have, in fact, to see the two parts of verse 16 in a much closer relationship with each other than it is usually possible to see them in most translations of the letter. The Greek word *opheilomen*, for example, means not only " we ought to " or " we must," but also " we are obliged to " or " we have the duty to," in this case, lay down our lives for our brothers. The same usage occurs in the passage in John 13 : 14, in which Jesus says not simply that " you also ought to wash one another's feet," but " you also are obliged to " or " have a duty to wash one another's feet."

What is more, the version of the commandment of love in 1 John 3 : 16 is also very closely related to that in John 15 : 12f. : " This is my commandment, that you love one another as I have loved you. Greater love has no man than this, that a man lay down his life for his friends." What distinguishes 1 John 3 : 16 from this passage in the gospel, however, is that what has to be inferred from John 15 : 12f. is made quite explicit in the letter—the love that the Christian has for his brother is the laying down of his life according to the norm of Christ's laying down of his life.

Moreover, the Christian's love of his brothers is a laying down of his life for them, *insofar as this is filled with Jesus' perfect renunciation of himself* (see Jn. 5 : 30). Everything that Jesus did was an expression of his obedience to the Father's commandment to lay down his life and the one great commandment which Jesus gave to his disciples was the commandment to love their brothers, so that they might respond more fully to his obedience to the Father. The brotherly love that Jesus wants us to have is an opening of our hearts, and this implies that our own will must die. This love is not possible for man to achieve himself. It presupposes the datum and the power of the cross.

THE CONFIDENCE THAT "GOD IS GREATER THAN OUR HEARTS"; OPEN AND CONFIDENT ASKING (3:19–22)

19By this we shall know that we are of the truth, and reassure our hearts before him 20whenever our hearts condemn us; for God is greater than our hearts, and he knows everything.

In these two verses we are again confronted with the author's great intention to stress the importance of our knowledge of our fellowship with God—"that we are of the truth [the divine reality]"—and, what is more, of our fellowship with God in spite of our sins. The phrase "whenever our hearts condemn us" undoubtedly refers to the sins that, according to 1:9, we are bound to confess. In this sense, then, 3:19f. must be regarded as a further contribution to the theme of "Christian and sin" and it must also have the same intention as the first and second expositions of this theme, namely, to strengthen Christians in their joy and confidence in salvation. Indeed, the underlying meaning of the verses 3:4-10, which, as we have seen, are at first sight so difficult to understand, emerges much more clearly on reading these two verses. We can appreciate now that the meaning of the earlier verses is to a very great extent based on the idea of God himself.

God is "greater than our hearts." This means that we are not expected to rely on our own strength. On the contrary, we are filled with the strength of the love of God and it is precisely for this reason that it is not the "knowledge" and the

" condemnation " or accusation of our own hearts that are ultimately decisive, but the fact that God knows " everything " by knowing us, in other words, by loving us (see Jn. 10:14f., 27).

Man's difficulties with regard to faith are probably different today from those of men living at the time when the letter was written. There was a deep consciousness of God then and consequently of man's sinfulness, with the result that the author's reference to the God who was " greater " indicated a cure from sinfulness. Nowadays, however, it is necessary to speak first of the God who is " greater " and to make man aware that he is really in the presence of God. Only then is it possible to go on to speak about a knowledge of sinfulness and to make the message of comfort which the letter contains meaningful to people today. I am, of course, oversimplifying the situation. Even contemporary man is conscious of disorder in his life and even he can be led to a consciousness of God through love. The idea of God presented by 1 John was, on the other hand, in no sense something which men living at that time simply took for granted.

²¹*Beloved, if our hearts do not condemn us, we have confidence before God;* ²²*and we receive from him whatever we ask, because we keep his commandments and do what pleases him.*

" Confidence before God "—having no fear in God's presence and being open to him—is *the* message of 1 John. He is not in the first place preaching human fellowship within this world. We should not, of course, underestimate this. Christians have often failed here, and it is no small achievement to lead them to human fellowship of the kind that is also attainable by non-Christians. On the other hand, however, our author could never be satisfied with this alone because he knew that it would not be fully in accordance with the reality of God and his revelation. What is more, his assurance that we should have no fear of and be open to God leads straight on to the statement that our prayers will be heard. Here too, as in the case of another, later statement of the author's intention, 5 : 13 (" I write this to you who believe in the name of the Son of God, that you may know that you have eternal life "), the affirmation is connected with the promise that God hears our prayers. This is a very great promise which will be fulfilled in the case of the man who keeps the commandments, that is, the commandments in which the one great commandment of love is expressed. Love is the condition on which our prayers will be heard and the man who loves will receive what he asks for in love. In John 14 : 12ff., faith in Jesus is the condition on which our prayers will be heard. In John 15 : 7, the condition is " abiding in Jesus." In the last resort, however, the author of 1 John is saying precisely the same, because we read later in the second passage in the gospel that abiding in Jesus, the true vine, is the same as abiding in his love, which is again the same as keeping his commandments and this means above all keeping the new commandment of love (see Jn. 15 : 9ff.).

Finally, at the end of verse 22, we read: " because we . . . do what pleases him." This statement should also not be regarded as Pharisaical, but as serving the whole message.

CONCLUSION: THE TWOFOLD ASPECT OF THE "COMMANDMENT" OF CHRIST; KEEPING THE COMMANDMENTS AND FELLOWSHIP WITH GOD (3 : 23–24)

[23]*And this is his commandment, that we should believe in the name of his Son Jesus Christ and love one another, just as he has commanded us.* [24]*All who keep his commandments abide in*

him, and he [God or Christ] in them [those who believe]. And
by this we know that he abides in us, by the Spirit which he has
given us.

In the first of these two verses, the Christian's obligation to
believe in Christ and his duty to love his brother are not seen
as two separate commandments or even as the only two commandments of real importance. On the contrary, they are combined closely together and regarded as *the* commandment of
God.

What does this imply? Is it possible that the two important
commandments are simply brought together here in a purely
formal way so that it will be clear to the reader that he cannot
do without either and that love, for example, is not sufficient in
itself without faith in Christ. (It might, after all, be possible to
conclude this from certain other parts of the letter.) Or has this
expression of *the* commandment of God, of the fact that love of
the brothers and faith in Christ together form only *one* commandment, to be taken quite literally?

A little later in the letter, in chapter 4, it is in fact made even
more obvious than it must already be here, as a result of our
analysis of various dimensions of the text so far, that the second,
the literal interpretation, is the only admissible one. It should
not be forgotten too, especially in considering this question,
that the " message " or " proclamation " which Christians have
" from the beginning " is, according to 1 John, both the content
of faith (" God is light," 1:5) and the commandment of love.
Thus, just as faith in the light of God's love as it reveals itself
to us and the commandment to love our brothers are simply two
aspects of the same proclamation, so too are the obligation to
believe in Christ and the duty to love simply two sides of the
same commandment. According to the Johannine way of thinking, there can be no faith in the love of God as it reveals itself

to us in Christ without the consequence of that faith, the believer's love of his brothers. On the other hand, the presupposition that is always present in the demand to love one's brothers is that the love of the Father was made known to man in Christ's laying down of his life.

We may go further and say that the author has by no means exhausted the theological and spiritual riches of this presentation of faith and love as the two sides of the one coin in this verse. His close combination of faith and love so as to show them as one single commandment is very strongly marked in the remaining two chapters of the letter. Indeed, one of his essential tasks in these concluding chapters is to link these two main themes of his letter even more strongly together.

God's Spirit has been mentioned twice before in the letter. The first time, the word " anointing " was used, and the second time the word " seed." Here, in the third reference to the Spirit, the word *pneuma*, Spirit, occurs for the first time, just as, in the preceding verse, 23, the word " believe " occurs for the first time in the letter. This also makes verse 23 an important transition to what follows. In the next part of the letter, a significant part is played by the word and the reality of the Spirit of God.

The Third Part of the Letter
(4:1—5:21)

Third Exposition of the Theme of "Faith in Christ" (4: 1–6)

At first sight, it would appear as though the transition between the preceding section and this one is as abrupt as in the case of the second exposition of the theme of " faith in Christ " (2: 18ff.) and as though a completely new beginning is made here as well. But, unlike 2: 17–18, there is in fact a clear link here. At the very least, the two sections are brought together by the use of the key word " Spirit " or *pneuma*. It is, however, not simply and solely a question of a key word forming the link, because there is already an echo of the theme of " faith " in 3:23—faith and love as God's commandment—and the Spirit, whom God has, according to 3:24b, given us, is certainly the power making love possible and, as the " anointing " of 2:20, 27, the teacher of faith and the power of faith.

¹Beloved, do not believe every spirit, but test the spirits to see whether they are of God; for many false prophets have gone out into the world. ²By this you know the Spirit of God : every spirit which confesses that Jesus Christ has come in the flesh is of God, ³and every spirit which does not confess Jesus is not of God. This is the spirit of antichrist, of which you heard that it was coming, and now it is in the world already.

According to the author of 1 John and indeed in the whole of the New Testament (see, for example, 1 Cor. 12), those who proclaimed a religious message were in the service of a spirit. Either the " spirit of truth " or the " spirit of error " was speaking from them in this case (4:6). Nowadays, we would probably say : test those who are proclaiming the message to see whether the " Spirit of God " or the " spirit of antichrist " is speaking through them (v. 3). But our author gives the concrete cause for his warning in 4:1ff. in verse 1b. Just as he spoke about " many antichrists " in 2:18, so too does he refer here to " many false prophets." They are, of course, the same people. We saw in 2:22f. that they denied the messianic character of Jesus and the fact that he was the Son of God and here, in 4:2f., we are told even more clearly what distinguishes them from the Christian community.

Every man who proclaims the true Christian message and

indeed every Christian confesses Jesus Christ as the one who " has come in the flesh " (v. 2). Christ is not a purely spiritual being as the gnostics believed, nor is he simply a cipher for something which corresponded to a gnostic idea of emanating in the physical sense from God. He is, on the contrary, a real man, so real that he was able to lay down his life. (This theme that Jesus came in the flesh is resumed in 5 : 6ff., where the author says that he came " by water and blood "; he is also proclaimed as coming in the flesh in 2 John 7.)

In the third verse of our section, the author simply says: " every spirit which does not confess Jesus." According to him, then, to confess Christ was fundamentally to confess the incarnate Jesus.

It should also be noted that Jesus did not, according to 1 John, come into the flesh—he came " in the flesh." In contrast to God, to whom the creative power of the Spirit is inherent, " flesh " indicates here, as it so often does in the Bible, the weakness and transient character of the creature. Unlike the Jews, the gnostics must have felt deeply outraged by the Christian teaching that the divine Logos not only penetrated into the darkness of matter, so as to release sparks of light from it, but also united itself so completely with the weakness of this " flesh." Jesus Christ came in the flesh : this means that the whole work of salvation which he set out to accomplish was determined by his close union with " flesh." It also includes the fact that he laid down his " flesh " for the life of the world.

As a norm by which the " spirits " can be distinguished, 1 John 4 : 1–3 can be interpreted very wrongly and, in the course of the history of the Church, it has frequently been so wrongly interpreted that the consequences have sometimes been disastrous. The most common cause of misinterpretation has been complete satisfaction with the non-violation of the orthodox confession of faith. In fact, however, a " spirit " is only " of

God " if the incarnation of the Logos and its consequences, man's *obligation to love,* are proclaimed by that spirit. In testing the spirits, what has to be asked is whether man is confirmed in selfishness or whether he is opened to love, the love that comes from God, by these spirits. It would indeed be valuable to test the various influences to which modern man is so exposed to see whether in fact they lead him towards selfishness and away from the love and service of his fellow men and whether they tend to make him less capable of expressing the love of God which is given to him as a Christian.

⁴Little children, you are of God, and have overcome them; for he who is in you is greater than he who is in the world. ⁵They are of the world, therefore what they say is of the world, and the world listens to them. ⁶We are of God. Whoever knows God listens to us, and he who is not of God does not listen to us. By this we know the spirit of truth and the spirit of error.

Here, the author says to his people: " You have overcome the false prophets," but at once the doubt arises as to whether a desire to " overcome " the false teachers is the proper Christian attitude. But the text does state, not " you can overcome them," but " you have overcome them." In the author's view, did his Christians possibly overcome the false teachers in some way which was not directed against them personally as people? How did they in fact achieve this victory? Did they succeed by an " orthodox " confession of Christ only or also in the way in which Christians overcame the " evil one " according to 2:13f.? The author of our letter regarded, as we have seen, these false prophets as forming a unity with the evil one. Is it perhaps not true to say that he had a " victory " by love and a " victory " by confessing Christ in mind, and that these also formed a unity for him?

The Christians have " overcome " the teachers of error because he " who is in them " is greater than he " who is in the world." This reference to the God who is " greater " can only, of course, be interpreted in the light of 3 : 19f. God is " greater " than his opponent, the " prince of this world " who is " in the world," because he is, as we know, light and love, and because the revelation of his love by Jesus and the power of the love that he pours into the hearts of those who believe in him through the Spirit are victorious. Christians are therefore victorious over the gnostic teachers of error because they have decided in favor of a " being of God," in other words, in favor of faith in Christ as faith in love.

When in verse 5 we read that the false prophets are " of the cosmos " or the world, this of course means, in the Johannine sense, that they are " of the darkness " in which real love is unknown. Their prophesying cannot, then, be any different from what it is and all that they can have at their disposal are the powers and the distorted norms of knowing which are inherent to this " darkness." The phrase " and the cosmos listens to them " accordingly implies that the Christian must also, especially when he is proclaiming the Christian message, test himself to see whether he is perhaps being well received by his listeners because what he himself is saying is " of the cosmos " and he is not shocking the " darkness " through the " light " of the " truth."

In verse 6, the author—or the group of which he was a member—says simply : " We are of God " and goes on to claim that everyone who is also of God listens to him. Is this a form of " clerical " presumption? There can be no doubt that this kind of statement has often given rise to such accusations during the course of the history of the Church. But there is a fundamental difference between clerical presumption as it has occurred (and perhaps still occurs) in the history of the Church and the reason underlying our author's statement. He is not making an infallible pronouncement concerning detailed aspects of Christian teaching here, declaring, in other words, that man's salvation depends on his listening and consenting to certain doctrines. No, he is above all concerned with the central reality of Christianity itself.

This consciousness on the author's part is clearly not based on dogmatic orthodoxy, but on his experience of the powerful effect and inspiring influence of the Spirit of God who urges Christians to acts of love. Christians have a criterion by which they can measure the reliability of their teacher (in this case, the author of 1 John): the extent to which they " know " God and love him and each other. It is possible for Christians to distinguish between the " spirit of truth " (the divine reality) and the " spirit of error " by testing their own love of God and its visible expression, their love of their brothers. If those who deny the incarnation of Christ oppose love because they deny the love of God as it has been revealed in Christ, then the " spirit of error " is identical with the spirit of hatred and the " spirit of truth " (the divine reality revealing itself in the Son's laying down of his life) is identical with the spirit of love.

Third Exposition of the Theme of the "Commandment of Love" (4 : 7–21)

If it is at all possible to say that one section of the letter contains its essence and climax, then it is in this section. It is the climax and the heart of the whole letter because of the statement " God is love " (4:8, 16). Perhaps the real central point, however, is the author's explicit combination of faith and love in verse 16a (faith in love); it is here that the unity of the letter can be most clearly recognized.

THE STATEMENT "GOD IS LOVE" AND ITS ELUCIDATION (4: 7–10)

⁷Beloved, let us love one another; for love is of God, and he who loves is born of God and knows God. ⁸He who does not love does not know God; for God is love. ⁹In this the love of God was made manifest among us [in us], that God sent his only Son into the world, so that we might live through him. ¹⁰In this is love, not that we loved God but that he loved us and sent his Son to be the expiation for our sins.

The first word in this section is " beloved " and this is followed by " let us love." In *this* particular section, which is so dominated by the idea of the love of God, this word " beloved " can hardly be simply the usual form of address. Clearly, it has less the sense of "my beloved ones " here and must rather mean " loved by God." It is only when we accept this meaning of the word that we can recognize the extent to which the following imperative " let us love " results here quite explicitly from an indicative, a conviction of faith—" because you are loved by God, love each other!"

This word " beloved " includes almost everything that the author wishes to tell us in the verses that follow about God's love for us. This interpretation of the word is, moreover, confirmed by 4: 11: " Beloved, if God so loved us "—words which certainly sound very much like an elucidation of the first word " beloved." Even the other three passages in the letter in which the address " beloved " occurs (2: 7; 3: 21; 4: 1) do not simply form links with the preceding passages in the purely technical sense, since in each case the previous passage is in some way concerned with God's love for us. Before 2: 7, for example, we find the statement: " in him truly love for God is perfected ";

before 3:21, we read "God is greater than our hearts"; and the key phrase "he abides in us" precedes 4:1.

Love is "of God." This is, of course, not the culminating statement about God contained in the letter. That is "God is love," which follows in the next verse. But this climax is certainly presupposed in the preliminary statement that we have here in verse 7, in which we are told that we should love each other because love comes from God and unites us with God. "Love is of God" is a very familiar phrase to us today, but for the author of our letter and for those who heard or read it for the first time, it denoted a powerful creative force. Whatever was "of God" was bound to be strong, creative, and divine.

"Let us love, because love is of God"; we are told to make the power that comes from God, love, effective! One of the reasons for this demand that we should love each other is to be found, of course, in the second half of verse 7: ". . . because he who loves is born of God and knows God." The author does not mean to say here, let us love each other so that *we ourselves may* fulfill the condition necessary to our being children of God and to our knowing God. No, what he is saying is, rather, let us love each other because it is only in this way that we can correspond to what we are *according to God himself*. The author's point of departure, in other words, is not man, but God.

The love of God was made manifest, these verses tell us, in the mission of his only Son, that is, in God's giving his Son, in death, as the expiation or atonement for our sins. The statement "God is love," then, does not refer to some proof of God's love in the abstract, but to this incomprehensibly great and concrete act of love. "God is love" means simply, he is the one who gave his Son for us in death. We find confirmation in verses 10a and 19 that this is precisely what is meant by the statement "God is love." Both of those texts tell us that the love discussed by the author of 1 John is not our love for God, but the love which God had for us in sending his Son to die for us. According to verse 19, God *first* loved us; it was not we who began to love, but he. The statement " God is love " is expressed in a way which leaves no possibility of misunderstanding in 4 : 10 and 4 : 19, in both of which we read that God loved us first.

We may conclude, then, by saying that " God is love " means that God is the love which is made manifest to us in Christ. It does not, for example, mean that God is " benevolence," " goodness," or " kindliness." No, he is love as total giving, and we may perhaps even go so far as to say, in the Johannine sense, that he is love as a total giving of himself, in that he gave his only Son for us. Although he always remains the same, he gives or pours himself away. He is the giving away of undiminishing infinity.

The final clause in this verse, ". . . so that we might live through him," indicates the way in which the effect of God's love in Christians is distinguished from its mission in the world. God sent his Son *into the world* so that *we* could be born of God —so that we might " know " God—and so that we might have fellowship with God. This means, in other words, that he sent his Son into the world so that we might be born *of love* and " know " *love,* because it is of love that the only life which really merits the name of life and which contains the promise made in 3 : 1f. consists.

BROTHERLY LOVE AS MAN'S RESPONSE TO THE LOVE OF GOD (4:11–13)

[11]Beloved, if God so loved us, we also ought to [are obliged to] love one another. [12]No man has ever seen God; if we love one another, God abides in us and his love is perfected in us. [13]By this

we know that we abide in him and he in us, because he has given us of his own Spirit.

The demand that we should love each other which was made in verse 7 is renewed in verse 11. It is, moreover, made more strongly here, and this is possible because the precise nature of the love to which our love of our brothers is to be a response has been made completely clear only in verses 7b–10. When the author says " no man has ever seen God," he is, of course, replying to the gnostics' claim to be able to come into direct contact with God. In opposition to their teaching, he maintains firmly that this direct contact—" seeing "—is not possible in this world and in this era (see also 3:2). There is, however, the possibility of extremely close contact with God, of a very close fellowship with God—a fellowship which the gnostics could not have—and this is that God " abides in us " if we love each other. In that case, God's love for us is " perfected in us."

This reference to " perfected love " should, of course, be compared with the previous passage in which it occurred (2:5). As in 2:5, so here too it means not an intensification of our own human capacity to love, but that God's love is perfected in us insofar as he—who is personal and perfected love—" abides " in us. We find the conclusion to this idea in verse 13, in which we read that God's love is perfected in us insofar as his Spirit, the power of " perfected love," abides in us.

Nowadays, we are much more able to perceive that a very real love and total giving of oneself in service of others exists in the world outside the Christian revelation than earlier generations of Christians. We can, in fact, no longer deny this fact which has been established according to non-Christian human criteria. But this undeniably real human, worldly love is not the " perfected love " of 1 John which God, according to our author, makes effective in us. It is an essential aspect of Christian faith that God introduced this love of total self-surrender (this "laying down" of one's life in love) into the world through Jesus' total surrender of his life (the "laying down of his life"), in such a way that he himself became manifest as love. If we are not therefore willing to let our own purely human image of the nature of love which gives itself totally be destroyed again and again by the revealed love of the God who is always "greater," and if we refuse to allow him to break down the barriers that we are so fond of erecting, then our understanding of love will never be the same as that of 1 John.

SECOND COMBINATION OF THE THEMES OF "FAITH" AND "LOVE" (4:14–16)

14And we have seen and testify that the Father has sent his Son as the Saviour of the world. 15Whoever confesses that Jesus is the Son of God, God abides in him, and he in God. 16So we know and believe the love God has for us [in us]. God is love, and he who abides in love abides in God, and God abides in him.

The theme of faith in Christ is reintroduced here, apparently very abruptly, by the solemn formula used at the opening of the letter: "We have seen and testify . . ." We know, of course, that the author's aim at the beginning of the letter was to testify to the "manifestation" of the love of God. It is quite obvious that this new testimony to faith in Christ is connected with the author's previous exposition of the love of God, because he speaks here in verse 14, as he did in verses 9 and 10, of the mission of the Son. God "has sent his Son as the Saviour of the world," we read here, and this is precisely the same as the proclamation made in verse 9: "God sent his only Son into the world" or cosmos "so that we might love through him." He sent him to

atone for our sins (v. 10). This simply means that he sent him
to reveal his love. It is precisely to this that the author and the
circle of witnesses to which he belonged wanted to testify,
because they had " seen " it.

The *content* of the confession of Christ in verse 15 emerges
not only from the verse itself, but also from the preceding verse.
It is, in other words, the same as the content of the testimony
that the Father sent his Son as the Saviour of the world. This is
in turn also the same as the statement made in verses 9 and 10,
namely, that the love of God is revealed in his sending his Son
so that he should die to atone for our sins. The statement " God
is love " is unimaginable without the accompanying idea of the
Son's mission and saving death, and, for this reason, faith in
Christ's mission and death—faith in Christ in the Johannine
sense—is identical with faith in God as love. Faith in Christ,
then, and faith in God as love both lead to the same conclusion:
man's obligation to love his brothers.

Moreover, faith in Jesus is not simply the " condition " for
faith in God's love for us; it *is* faith in God's love for us. In this
chapter of 1 John, the author has clearly concentrated on the
essential aspect of faith and, in so doing, it did not occur to him
that faith could contain anything else apart from love.

The second climax of this chapter occurs in the sentence,
" we know and believe the love God has for us," where it is
not purely fortuitous that the word " believe " is preceded by
" we know." It is true, of course, that, in the Johannine writings,
" knowing " and " believing " often seem to be simply two
aspects of the same event. But the word " know " is used so
frequently in 1 John with quite a distinctive meaning that this
special usage cannot be ignored in this case.

The object of faith, what we believe in, is, of course, the same
as the object of our testimony and our confession. This is why
what we, according to verse 16a, believe in (the love that God

has for us or " in us ") is materially a parallel to that to which witness is, according to verse 14, borne (that the Father has sent his Son as the Saviour of the world) and to what we, according to verse 15, confess (that Jesus is the Son of God). In the same way, it is also materially parallel to 4:2f. (the confession that Jesus Christ has come in the flesh) and to 3:23 (faith in the name of the Son of God).

Faith in the love that God has for us (or " in us "), then, includes all these various aspects of faith in Christ. This parallelism, especially that between the faith of verse 16a and the testimony and confession of verse 14f., shows clearly enough that, for the author of 1 John, faith in Christ was faith in the love of God. By bearing witness to the mission of the Son, the group of witnesses mentioned in 4:14 and previously were also testifying to the love of God or to God as love.

LOVE AND FEAR (4:17–18)

[17]In this is love perfected in us, that we may have confidence for the day of judgment; because as he [Christ] is, so are we in this world. [18]There is no fear in love, but perfect love casts out fear. For fear has to do with punishment, and he who fears is not perfected in love.

The compressed statement about faith in love in verse 16a seemed to contain everything that has to do with the Christian deposit of faith. One element, however, was not explicitly mentioned, and the author refers to it here. He attempts in this subsection to answer this question: Is the Christian's eschatological hope contained in this faith in the love that God has for us and in us? The situation of the Christian at the last judgment, which, according to Scripture, will take place at the end of time, is conditioned by this question.

The words " in this " at the beginning of verse 17 refer back to verse 16b. Love is perfected " with us " by our abiding in God and God's abiding in us, just as, in verse 12, " perfected love " is based on God's abiding in us. This perfected love (the " abiding " of God [in the sense of 4:8, 16] and of his Spirit in us, which brings about in us a love of our brothers) will also give us confidence on the day of judgment. (This may be compared with 3:20f., according to which the love of God who is " greater " enables us to be open and confident in our asking).

The clause " because as he is so are we in this world " (v. 17c), which provides the reason for this statement, is at first sight not at all easy to interpret. Does it point to the exemplary character of the life of Jesus in this world? If so, then it ought to be worded rather differently—we would expect " as he was " rather than the present tense. No, it refers to the glorified Christ, and the phrase " in the world " relates only to " us," not to Christ. The meaning, then, is: just as (the glorified) Jesus Christ *is* perfected in love, so too are we through him and through his " anointing," his Spirit, although we, unlike him, are still in this world.

It is also possible that the author was thinking of Christ as the judge on the future " day of judgment." This is a most impressive idea: we can be happy and confident on the day of judgment because the same love of God is active in us that is perfected in our Saviour, the judge of the world.

The opposite to the confidence which brings about love is, we learn in verse 18, fear of being put to shame and disgrace at the last judgment. (Verse 18 can be compared with 2:28: ". . . so that when he appears we may have confidence and not shrink from him in shame at his coming [parousia].") If we do not reassure our hearts when they accuse us (3:20), the accusation will be followed by this fear, which " has to do with punishment." Fear anticipates punishment, whereas love expects

the God who is " greater " and his mercy. Fear arises when
our hearts accuse us and this self-accusation is not subdued or,
as it were, " worked out " by trust in the God who is " greater."
This happens because " perfected " love (which is, in the first
place, the love which the Spirit of God brings about in us)
" drives out " fear. " There is no fear in love " because the love
which is of God contains only confidence. It cannot contain
fear if we allow it to prevail in us without restricting it in
any way.

The primary meaning of verse 18c is not that fear causes the
subjective love of the Christian to be expressed at a lower,
diminished level. It is, rather, that fear arises because the objec-
tive love of God is not able to be freely active in the Christian.
Once again, it is important to remember that the author of
1 John was taking as his point of departure not man but God.

LOVE OF GOD AND LOVE OF ONE'S BROTHER (4:19–21)

[19]*We love, because he first loved us.* [20]*If anyone says, " I love
God," and hates his brother, he is a liar; for he who does not
love his brother whom he has seen, cannot love God whom he
has not seen.* [21]*And this commandment we have from him, that
he who loves God should love his brother also.*

The idea contained in verse 10 is resumed in verse 19, but here
the author stresses the fact that God loved us *first*. We love
(or we practice love) because he loved us first. This does not
simply mean that we " respond to his love." Primarily, it means
that we are *able* to love because he has made a beginning,
because he has given us the power to love with his love.

The word " first " does, however, also contain the secondary
meaning that our love has the character of a response to God's

love. This knowledge is bound to be decisive to the Christian in his relationship with God. He will know that his love is not a sovereign action on the part of man, but on the one hand something that has been created by God and, on the other, his response or reaction. God, in other words, has the initiative here. This ought to be clearly demonstrated in how we pray to God. Our prayer, in other words, should in the light of this knowledge be in accordance with the datum of our relationship with God, and we should consequently not use as many words as possible, but rather listen to God himself in prayer. Whatever we may say or do is of its very nature a response to God's initiative.

In verse 20, the author makes it quite clear to us that what is meant in verse 19 cannot be a purely isolated divine love. It is, on the contrary, necessary for the love that God has given us to be handed on. But why is it that the man who does not love his brother cannot love God? And why should he be a " liar "?

According to 1 John, love is " in deed and in truth " (3 : 18), a love which is embodied in a " laying down of one's life." To some extent, what we have here is a conclusion " from the lesser to the greater." If the Christian does not take advantage of the first available opportunity to embody love, the author is saying, the opportunity that is " staring him in the face," but claims to have a " purely spiritual " love of God (which cannot, incidentally, be verified either by himself or by others and which exposes him to the grave danger of self-deception), then he is not simply not worthy of our faith; he is, in the author's strong term, a liar. Without love of one's brothers, any claim to love God is simply a lie.

The texts in which brotherly love is inseparably linked with the love of God are, in the last resort, above all an expression of the fundamental law of the incarnation. God who is invisible can be loved in human beings who are visible and this is possible only because the Son of God has come in the flesh and, as the prologue of John's gospel tells us (Jn. 1 : 12), he has given those who believe in him the power to become " children of God."

At the end of this passage, in verse 21, the commandment to love our brothers is expressed in a new way, namely, to show that the aim of the commandment is to link brotherly love with the love of God. It might, of course, be possible to read verse 20 and gain the impression that the author leaves it open as to whether it is really meaningful for man to love God directly. After reading verse 21, however, there can be no doubt that man's love of God is the first requisite of the commandment and that the author simply accepts without question that God must be loved. His intention here is to stress what was perhaps taken less for granted at the time, that not only God, but also one's brothers had to be loved in the power of God's love. We may in fact say that the author of 1 John does not in any way diminish the commandment to love God by throwing so much light on brotherly love here. On the contrary, he distills the message into its essential elements and still retains the full validity of the will of God as proclaimed in the Christian revelation.

Faith and the Testimony of God (5 : 1–12)

The theme of " love " reached its climax in chapter 4 and, what is more, it did so in combination with the theme of " faith in Christ." Our author, however, has more to say in connection with this second theme.

In the first place, he makes additional combinations between these two principal themes in this section (vv. 1 and 2–5, where he combines the themes of " faith in Christ," " being born of God," " love of God," " brotherly love," and " keeping the commandments "). In this context, the strongest emphasis that can be found in the whole letter is placed on faith, which is called the " victory that overcomes the cosmos." This is clearly an intensification and a culmination of the theme of victory which has already occurred in 2:12–14 and 4:4, and it should be noted that it was presupposed by the climax of the theme of love in chapter 4.

Secondly and from here, the author goes back to the themes that he touched on at the opening of the letter (1:1–4): " eternal life " is in the Son who has been made manifest to us and whom we can " touch " (vv. 11f.). The way to this is prepared by the statement about Jesus' " coming " in " water and blood " (v. 6ab)—this appears to be equivalent to the statements about the incarnation—and by the expositions of the " testimony " (the " three witnesses," vv. 6c–8, and the testimony of God, vv. 9–11).

This key word, " testimony " (*martyria*), which we have already encountered at the very beginning of the letter in 1:2, dominates the last verses of the body of the letter, which ends with this section. In fact, the words " witness," " testimony," and " testify " occur no less than ten times in 5:6–11 and they form the most powerful sound in the threefold final chord in the letter which is heard in this section. Two other words or phrases are also heard in this final chord: " victory " (or " overcome ") four times in vv. 4–5 and, at the very end of the section, " life " or " eternal life " four times in vv. 11f.

THIRD COMBINATION OF THE THEMES OF "LOVE" AND "FAITH IN CHRIST" (5:1–5)

¹Everyone who believes that Jesus is the Christ [Messiah] is a child of God [born of God], and everyone who loves the parent [the one—God—who has begotten] loves the child [the one who is born of him]. [2]By this we know that we love the children of God, when we love God and obey his commandments. [3]For this is the love of God, that we keep his commandments. And his commandments are not burdensome. [4]For whatever is born of God overcomes the world; and this is the victory that overcomes the world, our faith. [5]Who is it that overcomes the world but he who believes that Jesus is the Son of God?

Verse 1 consists of two halves, each beginning with "everyone" and each referring to the Christian. The first of the two clauses tells us what the Christian is (that he is "born of God") and the second tells us what he does (that he loves). The first halves of these two clauses are parallel with each other, in that they both consider the same object from the points of view of "faith" and "love" respectively, in other words, from the points of view of our by now very familiar themes. Verse 1a: Everyone who believes that Jesus is the Christ is born of God; verse 1b: Everyone who loves the one who has begotten (him) loves the one who is born of him (that is, his brother, who is also born of God).

In verse 2, however, there is a surprising change. Although this has the now familiar structure of a "knowing" formula, the object of our knowing is not our fellowship with God, but what has previously been our means of knowing: our love of our brothers. The usual parts of the Johannine "knowing" formula—the object of our knowing and our means of knowing—have clearly been transposed here. Why is this? Not only our fellowship with God and our love of him, but also the authenticity of our love of our brothers is problematical. It cannot simply be taken for granted and needs some guarantee against self-deception. This statement provides just such a safeguard. The authenticity of our brotherly love can be known by whether it is practiced not out of selfishness, but in obedience to the commandment of God, the commandment to imitate Christ's laying down of his life, that is, to give oneself totally in love. Our means of knowing whether our love of the children of God is genuine, then, is a love of God which is ready for active obedience.

This is reinforced in verse 3a. The love of God (which, in accordance with the context, here means above all our love of God, although this does not exclude the prior condition for this, God's love of us) does not consist of feelings and emotion, but in active obedience, the keeping of his commandment to love.

Verse 3b forms a transition to the culminating statement of this section—" and his commandments are not burdensome." We are, however, bound to ask why they are not difficult, and the answer, of course, is that the author was aiming to strengthen his Christians' certainty of salvation. This statement points in the same direction as those made in 3:4-10 and can be explained in the light of those statements. Further, God's commandments are not difficult because, as we read in verse 4a, everything that is " born of God overcomes the world," which means, of course, " everyone who is born of God." In everyone who is born of God there is the " seed " of God as the power of love which overcomes the " world "—in the sense that it is the sphere in which the " evil one " holds sway. In such a " world," a sphere of darkness where there is no love, faith in love is victory over the world of hatred and the absence of love.

The Content of the Testimony of the Spirit: The Coming of Christ "by Means of Water and Blood" (5:6)

[6]*This is he who came by water and blood, Jesus Christ, not with the water only but with the·water and the blood. And the Spirit is the witness, because the Spirit is the truth.*

What is the meaning of Jesus' coming " by water and blood "? In the first place, it is quite clear that this does not refer to Jesus' metaphysical being, but rather to his " having come," that is, to what he did for the salvation of the world.

In view of what we know about the attitude of the members of the Johannine circle (to which the author of 1 John certainly belonged) towards the baptism of Jesus in the Jordan, we are bound to conclude that no member of the Johannine circle would have characterized this event as a " coming with [or by means of] water."

There is, however, a further element that must not be overlooked. The fourth gospel does in fact speak about " water " in connection with Jesus, but this is not the water with which Jesus was baptized, but rather the water that he gives. In John 3:5, Jesus bestows new birth by water and the Holy Spirit, in other words, he baptizes with the Holy Spirit. In John 4, he gives " living water," the *pneuma* or " eternal life." In John 7:37-39, the water that flows from the body of Jesus is the eschatological gift of the Spirit.

Further, in 1 John 5:6, " water " and " blood " do not refer to two different saving events *within* the life of Jesus, because no separate event, apart from the incarnation itself, could be mentioned simultaneously with and in addition to Jesus' death on the cross and his exaltation. No, this " water " and " blood " together mean the *gift* which Jesus, together with the reality of the incarnation and the death on the cross, brings *through his " coming."*

The gift of " water " is therefore the lifegiving *pneuma*. The " blood " is the saving gift of expiation or atonement. There are above all not two quite different gifts here, the gift of " water " and the gift of " blood," but *one* gift, characterized by the author in two different ways: a gift that is lifegiving (the " water ") and at the same time expiatory (the " blood "). Both the term " water " *and* the term " blood " refer to the one gift of Jesus and that gift is the Holy Spirit.

This letter is dominated by such a carefully thought out, condensed theology that it would be impossible for every idea to be expressed within its restricted framework. Our task now, however, is to attempt to relate verse 6ab to this theology and especially to establish the extent to which it contributes to the whole of the author's theology of the *agape*.

" Jesus came by means of water and blood," then, is really a wider and deeper way of expressing Jesus' revelation and gift of the love of God by " water " and " blood." Let us look once again at the basic meaning of 5:5. The one who overcomes the world is the one who believes that Jesus is the Son of God, that is, the Son whom God has, according to 4:10, sent into the world to atone for our sins. (The concept " Son of God " must also has the same meaning in 4:15.)

Our verse, 6ab, in fact guarantees this faith in the love revealed in Christ against a serious misconception. Jesus " came " to save us not only by means of " water " (through the revelation of the Spirit), but also by means of " blood " (in his love of total self-surrender and in the power of that love). The " water " of the revelation of the Spirit is inseparably united with the " blood " of the love which gives itself totally. To conclude our attempt to elucidate the meaning of 1 John 6:5-6, then, a paraphrase may be helpful. Who is it who overcomes the world if it is not the man who believes in Jesus as the love of God in its self-revelation? It is Jesus who, by his coming, brings both revelation and atonement—not revelation only, but revelation (the communication of the Spirit) *and atonement* (which is the real and continuously active revelation of the love of God). (We may note in passing that " by blood " or " by means of blood " has more or less the same meaning as the " expiation " of 4:10.)

A clear connection is also discernible between verses 5 and 6 if the significance and power of Christ's " coming " as atonement are seen to be emphasized by the word " blood," and the full version of faith in Christ is seen to be a continuation of the thought in 4:9–10.

As far as verse 6c is concerned, the most important fact to note is that the key word " witness " (" tesify," " testimony "), which dominates the letter in these final verses of the third part before the conclusion of the letter as such, is prominent here. The *pneuma* or Spirit bears witness to this saving significance of Jesus (namely, that he has brought the power of the love of God in its self-revelation), because it is the " truth," that is, the *aletheia* or divine reality in its self-revelation, the Spirit of love.

THE THREE WITNESSES: THE "SPIRIT," THE "WATER" AND THE "BLOOD" (5:7–8)

[7]There are three witnesses, [8]the Spirit, the water, and the blood, and these three agree.

The *pneuma* bears witness—in verse 6c, this refers both to the proclamation of the word *and* to the sacrament, whereas in verse 8 it refers more to the proclamation of the word as the testimony of the Spirit. (In this proclamation of the word, the Spirit, as the " anointing," teaches us " about everything "—that is, the whole revelation of love; see 2:27.)

The " water " bears witness, when a person is publicly baptized in the Church, in other words, when he is " born of God " through faith and baptism, the " anointing " bears witness to the fact that God is here pouring his " seed " into this person as the love that reveals itself in the Son's laying down of his life. (It is less good to say that baptism bears witness here. It is clearly better to say that the Spirit given as " anointing " in baptism bears witness to the saving significance of the death of Jesus.)

The " blood " bears witness. When the Eucharist is celebrated in the Church (in the gospel of John, the concept " blood " is used almost exclusively in the eucharistic sense), the death of the Lord is proclaimed (see 1 Cor. 11:26). The eucharistic blood of the Son of man (John 6:53ff.), which can only be understood as the sacrificial blood of his death, bears witness to the fact that there can be eternal life only as the fruit of that death, that is, through the incarnation of the Logos which is completed in death. The blood which Jesus shed on the cross and which reveals the love of God communicates itself to us, through the Spirit which is active in the community of those who believe, in the sacrament of the Eucharist. The consequence of this is not only that it purifies us from sin as an obstacle to love, but also that it can continue to reveal and to bear witness to the love of God through us and in us.

The " three witnesses " may therefore be interpreted in the following way. The dominant concept is the " Spirit," which is seen here as the " anointing " which teaches us about everything and as the power of the proclamation of the word. The " water " points to the Spirit given to us in baptism as the " seed " of our being " children of God " and born of the love of God. The " blood " is the Spirit of brotherly love which assures us of our unity with each other in the Eucharist and which is expressed according to the norm set by Jesus in the laying down of his life.

" And these three agree," that is, they are united in the witness that they bear—a development of verse 6c, which tells us that the Spirit is the " testifying " one. Verse 8b completes this statement. The Spirit is also the " testifying " one in the " water " and the " blood."

The "Greater" Testimony of God (5:9)

⁹If we receive the testimony of men, the testimony of God is greater; for this is the testimony of God that he has borne witness to his Son.

The testimony of God is " greater " than that of men. Presumably the author is here speaking of the false teachers. Christians can gain a victory over them because God himself, who is " in them," is " greater " than " he who is in the world," that is, the evil one who speaks in these men (see 4:4). The clause " if we receive the testimony of men " shows clearly enough that the author was here taking the danger of his Christians accepting the teachings (the " testimony ") of the gnostics just as seriously into account as he was considering the real risk in 1:6ff. (" If we say . . .") of their believing, with the gnostics, that they were without sin.

" For this is the testimony of God that he has borne witness to his Son." In speaking here of the " Son " of God, the author must clearly have had in mind, as he did in 4:9f., 15, that the Father sent this Son to reveal his love by dying. The testimony of God is " greater " because it is the testimony of the " greater " love which has been proclaimed in the mission of the Son.

The Attitude of Man towards the Testimony of God (5:10)

¹⁰He who believes in the Son of God has the testimony in himself. He who does not believe God has made him a liar, because he has not believed in the testimony that God has borne to his Son.

We may paraphrase this verse thus: He who believes that God has this particular Son (whom he has sent to lay down his life for us), in other words, whoever believes in the love of God which has, according to 4:16a, been shown to us, has been poured into us and will continue to be active in us—that man has the testimony of God in him. Another possible paraphrase is: He who believes in the love that God has revealed in his Son has the " testimony of God " in him because he has, by faith (and " knowledge "), admitted love into his heart. He has the testimony of God in him because the " seed " and the " anointing " of God are in him, in other words, the *pneuma* of verse 6c (" and the Spirit is the witness . . ."). This is because the Spirit itself brings about the testimony of verses 9ff.—because it *is* basically this " testimony."

But how does the non-believer make God a liar? This question can only be answered by referring back to the other passages in which the words " liar " or " lie " occur (1:10; 2:22; 4:20).

According to the author of 1 John, who was not considering individual cases in the concrete, but only the fundamental structure of the realms of light and of darkness, the non-believer, as a consequence of his absence of faith, became a man who did not love. He not only denied all external testimony about Jesus, he also rejected everything that was within his reach through the activity of love in himself, through active love of his brothers.

But did our author mean by this reference in verse 10bc only the false teachers who were not members of the Christian community, or was he also including those who belonged to the community? 1:6–10 provides us with the answer. This parallel (and the use of the form " we ") makes it quite clear that even the Christian who belongs to the community of Christ cannot regard himself as immune from this danger.

The non-believer makes God a " liar," then, by not accepting him as perfect " light " and by not accepting the divine reality which reveals itself as love.

The Giving of Eternal Life as the Testimony (5:11–12)

[11]*And this is the testimony, that God gave us eternal life, and this life is in his Son.* [12]*He who has the Son has life; he who has not the Son of God has not life.*

The "testimony of God" is expressed again in verse 11, this time in a new way. Here it consists of God having given us "eternal life." This transition from verse 10 to verse 11 can only be meaningful if we think of "eternal life" in 1 John as signifying the life of love, life in God himself, who is love. The testimony that the believer has in him is the life that God has given him "in his Son," the life that God has given him by "begetting" him through his "seed."

God, then, has given us eternal life by giving us his love. The realm of "life" into which we have passed (see 3:14) is the realm of love, and we know by our love of our brothers that we are in the realm of life. What is more, we believe God when we believe the testimony of love which he transmits to us via his witnesses (see 1:1–4; 4:14) and which he has placed in us. "Being born of God" is in fact the same as "having life" and, since God is love, it is also the same as being born of love and the life of love.

The Conclusion of the Third Part and of the Whole Letter (5:13–21)

Does this concluding section present us with a really unified sequence of thought or not? This question has to be answered before we discuss the section in detail, because it will influence our interpretation of it. It is clear from the fact that this section is obviously in sharp contrast with the other sections in the letter either that the writer is aiming to come to a conclusion or that he regards the letter as already concluded. In verse 13, for example, he looks back at the letter and defines his purpose in writing it. In the second place, the individual themes which he discusses in this section also seem at first sight to be rather like supplements to the letter itself, elements with which the author is very much concerned, but which he has not yet been able to include in the body of the letter itself.

THE AIM OF THE LETTER: TO AROUSE CONFIDENCE IN SALVATION (5:13)

[13]I write this to you who believe in the name of the Son of God, that you may know that you have eternal life.

The author here states that he has written his letter to Christians (to those who " believe in the name of the Son of God ") so that they may know that they possess eternal life, that they may therefore live as Christians in happy confidence of salvation (see also above, 2: 12–14).

GOD'S HEARING OF OUR PRAYERS (5:14–15)

[14]And this is the confidence which we have in him, that if we ask anything according to his will he hears us. [15]And if we know that he hears us in whatever we ask, we know that we have obtained the requests made of him.

We have already encountered this " confidence " and the assurance that our prayers are heard by God in an important passage (3:2f.). In contrast to 3:21f., for example, this assurance contains the addition " according to his will." Is this a general theological safety clause, so that the promise that our prayers will be heard cannot be misused, or did the author have a definite resolution on the part of God in mind? The answer to this question is provided in the verses that follow, but especially in verse 16.

THIRD EXPOSITION OF THE THEME OF "CHRISTIAN AND SIN" (5:16–17)

[16]*If anyone sees his brother committing what is not a mortal sin, he will ask, and he will give him life for those whose sin is not mortal. There is a sin which is mortal; I do not say that one is to pray for that.* [17]*All wrongdoing is sin, but there is sin which is not mortal.*

As we have already seen, "mortal sin" was, for the author of 1 John, hatred of one's brothers, the fundamental decision made against the light of love and in favor of darkness (which is at the same time and primarily a decision against faith in Christ as faith in the love of God in its self-revelation). Our author, however, also insists very emphatically in verse 17 that there is also a "sin which is not mortal." It was important for him to insist on this in his controversy with the gnostics. This "sin that is not mortal" is the sin which Christians are urged to confess in 1:9 and of which their hearts accuse them in 3:20. By refusing to accept these sins and their atonement through Christ, the gnostics become involved in the darkness.

The final sentence of verse 16: "There is a sin which is mortal; I do not say that one is to pray for that" is very difficult for us to understand. It is true that the author is not forbidding us to pray for those in "mortal sin," but it seems extremely hard of him even to raise the question. Are we to attribute to him a view of predestination that was totally conditioned by his own historical period?

The answer to this question is to be found in the fact that

his view was determined by his theological preoccupation with the " evil one." It was in the light of this " evil one " that he judged all those who had put themselves under his sway. We, on the other hand, are inclined now to consider individual people in the concrete and to regard man as an arena in which light and darkness are struggling for mastery. We may regret that our author says nothing that would appeal directly to us as twentieth-century men, but we should remember that what he in fact says expresses the attitude of a man of his period and a Christian to whom light and darkness were irreconcilably opposed to each other.

"Knowledge" of Salvation (5:18–20)

18We know that anyone born of God does not sin, but he who is born of God keeps him, and the evil one does not touch him. 19We know that we are of God, and the whole world is in the power of the evil one. 20And we know that the Son of God has come and has given us understanding, to know him who is true [the real one]; and we are in him who is true [in the real one], in his Son Jesus Christ. This [one] is the true [real] God and eternal life.

In verses 18–20, we have the threefold concluding emphasis, " We know . . .", that I have already referred to above.

Verse 18: This first sentence beginning with the phrase " We know . . ." is still within the framework of the theme of verses 16–17—that of " Christian and sin." It is a triumphant repetition, made in the certainty of Christ's victory, as outlined in 3:4–10, of the conviction that he who is born of God, that is, of personal love, does not fall into sin (in the sense, of course, of fundamentally not loving and of satanic hatred). Here, however, the author gives a further reason for this, in addition to what he has said previously in the letter (3:4-10): God preserves the one who is born of him, so that the evil one cannot touch him.

Verse 19: This second " We know . . ." throws a very power-ful light, once again, on the great contrast between Christians, who can be sure of their salvation because they are " of God," that is, because they are children of God and have fellowship with him, and the " world," which is the sphere in which the " evil one," God's adversary, holds sway. The whole of the " world," our author insists, is in the power of the " evil one." As in the case of 2:15-17, we can only recognize that this pas-sage points beyond a purely dualistic view of the kind encoun-tered, for example, in the Qumran texts to a much broader and deeper insight, if we try to see it within the whole context of the central message of the letter itself. The author believed that the whole world was in the grip of darkness and the coldness of not loving and urgently needed the revelation of God's love and fellowship with that love if it was to enter the clarity and the warmth of light. He was also convinced that *we* have been given the ability to pass from the realm of death into the realm of life (see 3:14) and that we know this in faith.

Verse 20: In this third statement introduced by " We know . . .", the author again leads us very deeply into his essential theological message concerning God and his Son. " We know . . .", he tells us, " that the Son of God has come . . ."— that he has come in the reality of the " flesh " (4:2), not simply as a pneumatic gift, a spiritual gift, but above all with his expiatory blood (5:6). He has given us " understanding " to know " him who is true," that is, the " real one," the divine reality in its self-revelation, God himself, and thus to enter into fellowship with love itself. This " understanding," however, has been given to us by Jesus Christ, who is not simply a teacher and prophet, but the Son of God, the Holy One, the " anointed " one. What is more, he has given us this " understanding " through the anointing that we have from him (2:20, 27).

The author concludes this section with a terse statement which shows us the reason for the power that the Son of God can claim to have for us: we do not simply " abide " in God, but " are " also in his Son, and this Son is so intimately united with the Father that he can also be called, like the Father, the " real one." Then, once again with an almost shocking terseness, the author gives us a summary of his Christology: " this [one] is the ' real ' God and eternal life." This is a statement which could, in the New Testament, have been expressed in this form only as a Johannine thought. Its basis is to be found in John 14:9f.: " He who has seen me has seen the Father." As the one who reveals his love, the Son is so completely open to the Father that whoever sees him also sees the Father, God himself, and can speak to God in him.

FINAL WARNING (5: 21)

[21]*Little children, keep yourselves from idols.*

This particular concluding sentence is surely almost entirely unexpected. Nothing has been said so far about " idols " throughout the whole text of the letter. But we do know from the Qumran texts that " idols " were, at that time, very closely associated with the idea of sin as a power directed against God. If, then, at the time when our letter was written, " idols " were what drew men away from the true God and put themselves in his place, then this concluding statement becomes quite distinctly meaningful within the whole theological context of the letter. " Idols," we may conclude, therefore represent everything that tries to depose love (personal love) and to take its place in such a way that the result will be a complete absence of love and " hatred."

THE SECOND EPISTLE OF ST. JOHN

A brief analysis of the thought in 2 John as a whole is not out of place. The fundamental aim of the letter is expressed in verses 8ff., and most clearly in verses 1of. It is probable that it was feared that false teachers of the kind described earlier, in our discussion of 1 John, might find their way into the community and indeed that they might do this before the " elder " himself arrived. The "elder " wanted to prevent this from happening and therefore wrote this letter. His demand is that Christians should reject the false teachers.

With great tenacity of purpose, the author leads up to this fundamental warning or admonition. To begin with, he impresses on his readers the importance of the commandment of love, no doubt because he recognizes that it was absolutely necessary for the community to be quite united if the false teachers were to be repelled. After this, he contrasts the false Christological teaching of the gnostics with the true teaching about Christ. We have already encountered this kind of thinking in 1 John, where the commandment of love and Christology were combined (or where erroneous teaching concerning Christ was rejected).

The Opening of the Letter (vv. 1–3)

[1]*The elder to the elect lady and her children, whom I love in truth, and not only I but also all who know the truth,* [2]*because of the truth which abides in us and will be with us forever :* [3]*Grace, mercy, and peace will be with us, from God the Father and from Jesus Christ the Father's Son, in truth and love.*

Verse 1 : In the ancient epistolary form, the name of the writer of the letter appeared first. The writer of 2 and 3 John, however, did not put his name at the beginning of these letters, but called himself the *presbyteros* or " elder." This is, moreover, scarcely the title that a leader of our author's stature in the Church would give himself in New Testament times. As far as we know, the *presbyteroi* were, in the primitive Church, members of a college of " elders," whereas our author was clearly a very prominent personality with extraordinary powers. The inclusion of this title, *presbyteros*, at the opening of the letter instead of the more usual name of the writer can only be explained if its use gave those addressed, the particular community or the communities which came within the author's sphere of influence, the unmistakable impression that the writer was in fact this man of extraordinary importance.

The author tells the members of the Christian community to whom he is writing that he loves them " in truth." He does not do this as it were in an excess of emotion, but to express the fact that his relationship with the community is characterized by the bond of faith.

Verse 2 provides to some extent an answer to the question why *agape* is directed towards these Christians. The author tells us that this is because of the " truth " or *aletheia*, that is, the divine reality which reveals itself to the world and which " abides in us "—in other words, because this " truth " is not something purely external to the Christian and something which is merely an object of his knowing, but because it " is " and " abides " in him.

In verse 3, the author includes himself in the traditional Christian blessing: " Grace, mercy, and peace will be with *us* . . ." Although it is a traditional blessing, it is given a distinctively Johannine flavor by the ending " in truth and love " (in *aletheia* and *agape*). Clearly, the author means that grace, mercy, and peace will be given to Christians in the sphere of the divine reality in its revelation of itself and in love, the love which God himself is.

The Body of the Letter (vv. 4–11)

The Exhortation to Brotherly Love (vv. 4–6)

⁴I rejoice greatly to find some of your children following the truth, just as we have been commanded by the Father. ⁵And now I beg you, lady, not as though I were writing you a new commandment, but the one we have had from the beginning [from the origin], that we love one another. ⁶And this is love, that we follow his commandments; this is the commandment, as you have heard from the beginning, that you follow love [in him].

The author does not begin by exhorting his Christians to love each other, but first, in verse 4, expresses his happiness at finding that there is " walking in the *aletheia* " in the community. As we know from 1 John, this is, of course, materially the same as *agape*, so that what the author is really saying here is that there is already solidarity among the members of the community, but that they must be exhorted again and again and with renewed intensity to love their brothers. It is also clear, from what the author says in verse 7ff. about the danger to the community caused by the false teaching of the gnostics, that it was very necessary to stress this admonition to love. His encounter with the members of the community whom he is addressing (v. 4) provides him with an opportunity to say what he in fact says in verse 5f. and, what is more, this is made easier by the previous meeting referred to in verse 4. We may safely assume that this is not simply a suitable idea, expressed in the interests of Christian teaching, but that the author was sincerely overjoyed by what he had seen in the community and that he, either in spite of this or because of it, felt compelled to strengthen the members of the community in their will to love each other. The author also clearly takes the same view of the commandment (or " commandments ") here as he did in 1 John 2:7f., although the commandment is here described as " old " and not, as in the first letter, " new." Believers have this commandment of love from the " origin " of their status as Christians; they have it from the original and fundamental love of God and Jesus.

The True Confession of Christ as Opposed to the Teachings of the "Deceivers" (vv. 7–11)

WARNING AGAINST THE DOCTRINES OF THE FALSE TEACHERS (vv. 7–9)

⁷*For many deceivers have gone out into the world, men who will not acknowledge the coming of Jesus Christ in the flesh; such a one is the deceiver and the antichrist. ⁸Look to yourselves [take care], that you may not lose what you have worked for [what we have been striving to gain], but may win a full reward. ⁹Anyone who goes ahead and does not abide in the doctrine of Christ does not have God; he who abides in the doctrine has both the Father and the Son.*

Verse 7 says that " many deceivers have gone out into the world . . ." and this is clearly the same as " many antichrists " in 1 John 2:18. The word " antichrist " also appears at the end of our verse, 7, and, even more literally, " many false prophets " in 1 John 4:1. But in what way can this statement provide the reason for the request expressed in the preceding passage? This word " for " in fact refers back to the introductory words " and now " in verse 5, which stress the importance of exhorting Christians to love each other at *this* particular time. The " for " therefore gives the author's reason for the urgency to exhort believers at this point of time, precisely because there are so many false teachers who combine an " ethical lie " with a " Christological lie." We can express this more precisely, perhaps, in the following way. Our author's theological perspicacity enabled him to perceive very clearly the inner connection between the false teachers' denial of the incarnate Jesus Christ on the one hand and their own personal lack of *agape* or love on the other. He saw, in other words, that, by denying the love of God that he has shown in the real death of Jesus, these men were not able to have the radical *agape* that God wanted men to have for each other.

What is the meaning of the second of these remarkable facts, the use of the present tense to express the confession " that Jesus Christ *comes* in the flesh "? According to the Johannine way of thinking, the glorified Christ is also " in the flesh." He is still the individual man who was "exalted " on the cross and who still bears the wounds inflicted on him. His incarnation continues to be actively present in the lives of the disciples. He did not simply come " in the flesh " to the people in Palestine at that particular time; he also continues to come *to us,* not only in some mystical, pneumatic way, but " in the flesh." He comes to us in the Church, in which the human element is inseparably combined with the divine and in which men who are " in the flesh " are the instruments of Jesus as Kyrios. One element which is absolutely fundamental to the Catholic concept of the Church is that the principle of incarnation applies fully even to the Church in the present era.

The text of verse 8 has been handed down to us in two

versions, both of which are well substantiated and both of which provide good readings. The first version reads: take care " that you may not lose what you have worked for . . ."; and the second: ". . . that you may not lose what we have been striving to gain." The reason for this warning is to emphasize what follows in verse 9, and it can be paraphrased thus: anyone who does not keep to the rule outlined in verse 9 either risks losing the results of his own commitment to faith or else threatens to undermine the fruit of the missionary effort that has led him to faith.

The last verse in this subsection, verse 9, has a clear parallel in 1 John 2:23 and the reader should refer to our commentary on this passage. It is obvious that the author is warning his readers here against the tendency of the gnostics not to accept the teaching of the Church and not to " abide " in it, but to press forward and embrace completely new " pneumatic " speculations.

THE BAN ON OFFERING HOSPITALITY TO THE FALSE TEACHERS (vv. 10–11)

[10]*If anyone comes to you and does not bring this doctrine, do not receive him into the house or give him any greeting;* [11]*for he who greets him shares his wicked work.*

This apparently extremely hard attitude towards the false teachers is certainly the result of the circumstances prevailing at the time the letter was written. The gnostics constituted such a serious danger to the Christian community that the author of 2 John was convinced that the substance of faith could only be preserved if there was a radical division between them and Christians. What is more, the greeting that the members of the Christian community are forbidden to give was certainly more than a polite formula. It meant reception into a community and in this case the community of the Church.

But is this peremptory ban on all normal human relationships with the gnostics, which is undeniably expressed in the letter, simply something that was conditioned by and applies only to the historical circumstances at the time, or can it still have a meaning for Christians today? Each of us has to decide what attitude to take towards this question.

The Closing of the Letter (vv. 12–13)

[12]*Though I have much to write to you, I would rather not use paper and ink, but I hope to come to see you and to talk with you face to face, so that your or [or: our] joy may be complete.* [13]*The children of your elect sister greet you.*

In verse 12, our author makes it clear that he has not by any means said everything that he wanted to say to the community and that he wants to make up for this in personal contact so that their " joy may be completed." The parallel with 1 John 1 : 4 is obvious and we may assume that, in both cases, this " joy " is evoked by the *proclamation* and " completed " by it. Certainly, the author does not mean here that joy will be " completed " by the personal touch of speaking " face to face." No, he is here referring to the content of the " proclamation " and this is, from our study of verses 4–11, clearly the same as in the first letter: the message of the *agape* of God incarnate in Jesus.

THE THIRD EPISTLE OF ST. JOHN

The ideas contained in 3 John can be summarized as follows. The whole letter can be said to be concerned with the reception or rejection of strange " brothers," and this theme is present even where it is not explicitly stated. These strangers are travelling missionaries who were obviously sent out by the " elder," the author of the letter, who was in turn very interested in their activity and in their possible influence. In part 1 of the letter, Gaius is both praised for his attitude towards these missionaries and is also asked to equip them to continue their work. In part 2, it is the activity of these missionaries which forms the substance of the conflict between the " elder " and Diotrephes. Finally, part 3 contains a commendation of Demetrius, who was in all probability also a travelling preacher and perhaps even the leader of the group.

The Opening of the Letter (v. 1)

¹The elder to the beloved Gaius, whom I love in the truth.

This is the shortest greeting in the whole of the New Testament. It is completely in accordance with other greetings of this period, but the conclusion is distinctively Johannine: " whom I love in the truth."

The Body of the Letter (vv. 2–12)

Praise of Gaius and Request to Support the Missionaries (vv. 2–8)

²Beloved, I pray that all may go well with you and that you may be in health; I know that it is well with your soul. ³For I greatly rejoiced when some of the brethren arrived and testified to the truth. ⁴*No greater joy can I have than this, to hear that my children follow the truth.* ⁵*Beloved, it is a loyal thing you do when you render any service to the brethren, especially to strangers,* ⁶*who have testified to your love before the church. You will do well to send them on their journey as befits God's service.* ⁷*For they have set out for his sake [for the name] and have accepted nothing from the heathen.* ⁸*So we ought to [are obliged to] support such men, that we may be fellow workers in the truth.*

In verse 2, the author expresses the wish that Gaius is prospering " in everything " (" that *all* may go well ") and sees this wish fulfilled in the most important respect: he knows that " it is well with your soul." In this he is obviously alluding to Gaius' " walking in the *aletheia* " (vv. 3ff.).

For the author's joy that Gaius is " walking in the *aletheia* " (vv. 3–4), the reader should refer back to the exegesis of 2 John 4 and especially of 1 John 1:6—2:6.

Verses 5–8: Gaius' attitude towards the travelling missionaries which is praised here is undoubtedly not a special case of " walking in the *aletheia*," but rather an indication as to how this should be understood in the context of this passage. According to the author, " walking in the sphere of the divine reality in its self-revelation [*aletheia*]" cannot exist without cooperating with this process of revelation, in other words, unless the Christian is a " fellow worker in the *aletheia*." Our author also believed that the individual Christian's ethical " walking in love " was also orientated towards this cooperation and was not " missionary " unless it was given a directly missionary aim.

As in the case of 2 John 4f., the author here expresses praise and a request at the same time. Gaius has already committed himself generously to the cause of the preachers whom the

" elder " has sent out, but the " elder " clearly expects this commitment to be lasting and perhaps even fuller. He therefore asks Gaius to equip the " brothers " so that they can continue their missionary journey (v. 6b). Verses 7 and 8 to some extent provide a reason for this request: the " brother," the author says, set out for the " name," that is, for the name of Christ.

We must think of the " name " here as meaning the same as the *aletheia* in the following verse, 8, in other words, as the reality of God which can be named in Jesus and can be proclaimed in the work of gaining converts. The missionary brothers, we are told, " have accepted [or received] nothing from the heathen." This is either because they did not expect or wish to be supported by the pagan people who were not yet converted to Christianity or else—and this is more likely— because they did not want to accept anything from the non-Christian people who heard the message they were proclaiming so as to make that message more worthy of belief. The result is, in either case, that the missionaries had to rely on the support of Christians who already believed. Verse 8 even refers to an obligation or duty to support these missionaries. This obligation is clearly the result of the fact that no one can be a Christian in the full sense of the word unless he is a " fellow worker in the *aletheia*."

The Conflict with Diotrephes (vv. 9–10)

[9]*I have written something to the church; but Diotrephes, who likes to put himself first, does not acknowledge my authority.* [10]*So if I come, I will bring up what he is doing, prating against me with evil words. And not content with that, he refuses himself to welcome the brethren, and also stops those who want to welcome them and puts them out of the church.*

Diotrephes seems to have been a leader in the Church community to which Gaius also belonged and he may even have been the leader of the community itself. According to verse 9, the " elder " clearly regarded him not only as personally ambitious, but also as having a high opinion of himself in the office which he occupied (he " likes to put himself first "). The " elder," however, conscious of his superior position, aimed to call him to account (v. 10a). Both the letter written by the " elder " to the community, which Diotrephes did not acknowledge—as he also failed to acknowledge the " elder's " authority generally—and the hard things that Diotrephes was saying about the " elder " are, we may be quite sure, connected with this clearly ambitious and conceited man's attitude towards the missionary " brothers." The real bone of contention, then, is that Diotrephes was preventing these men, who had been sent out by the " elder," from carrying out their missionary work and was even trying to expel from the community those who gave them accommodation.

The Commendation of Demetrius (vv. 11–12)

[11]*Beloved, do not imitate evil but imitate good. He who does good is of God; he who does evil has not seen God.* [12]*Demetrius has testimony from everyone, and from the truth itself; I testify to him too, and you know my testimony is true.*

Verse 11 marks the transition. Neither " evil " nor " good " is seen in the abstract here, as in the case of 1 John, but both are made fully concrete in the " missionary " sense or even in the sense of " Church politics."

Verse 12: Even the theme of " testifying," which is so familiar to us from the gospel of John and from the first letter, is made concrete here in the sense of testifying " to Demetrius." Do we perhaps find, in verse 12, a concept of " testimony " which cannot be reconciled with the more abstract idea in 1 John? It is obvious that, whereas witness was borne in the fourth gospel and in 1 John to the saving activity of Jesus himself, what we have here is an apparently " profane " testimony to an individual within the Christian community. This may, of course, indicate that we are perhaps not dealing with the same author as the writer of John 15 : 35, but with a man who was familiar with the terminology of the writer of John 15 : 35, but who used it differently. It is, on the other hand, not impossible that the same man decided himself to use the concept of " testimony " in a more concrete way. This would only be completely out of the question if the author of the gospel or, even more, of 1 John were not in a position to consider the whole reality of Christian life together with all its concrete forms and expressions, which are above all those forms in which the *aletheia* of the divine reality in its self-revelation through Jesus (see, for example, Jn. 5 : 7ff.) is active. Both in John 19 : 35 and in John 5 : 7ff., the author is speaking of the testimony of the activity of the Spirit in the era of the Church—and the activity of a Christian missionary such as Demetrius indisputably forms a part of this. What is more, as the author points out, the witness of which he is speaking here is not borne simply and solely by men, but " from the truth itself," in other words, it is borne by Jesus, who lives with God and is active through the Holy Spirit.

The Closing of the Letter (vv. 13–15)

¹³I had much to write to you, but I would rather not write with pen and ink; ¹⁴I hope to see you soon, and we will talk together face to face.¹⁵Peace be to you. Greet the friends, every one of them.

Personal proximity, the desire to see one's friends again and be with them, is not contrary to serving the truth. The letter gains a little warmth from this concluding greeting, despite the fact that it is otherwise rather formal, like the conclusion to 2 John. But even something that is repeated in the same form in two different letters need not lack authenticity.

THE EPISTLE OF ST. JUDE

INTRODUCTION

The Self-Defense of a Troubled Community

1. The author of the short letter of Jude was not by nature a fighting man. His whole purpose was to write about the salvation offered to all (v. 3). His delight was in meditating upon the truths of faith and grouping them in short, thought-provoking units. It is not by chance that things occur in three's in his letter: the blessings of salvation are mercy, peace, and love (2); the great religious treasures of the Christian are prayer in the Holy Spirit, the mercy of our Lord Jesus Christ, and perseverance in the love of God (20); eternity is thought of as unending past, present, and future (25); the one God is tri-personal (20); threat of divine retribution is signalled by the wandering in the desert, the fall of the angels, and the destruction of Sodom and Gomorrah (5–7); biblical prototypes of false teachers are Cain, Balaam, and Korah (11).

This man, for whom the " most holy " blessing of the faith was his love and joy, saw himself opposed by false teachers, the so-called gnostics. Recent research into gnosis has revealed its fascinating attraction and its disruptive effect within the Christian community. The letter of Jude sums up the perversion of the gnostics in three striking phrases: they " defile the flesh, reject authority, and revile the glorious ones " (8). What is most sacred is no longer considered sacred at all. Ingenious word-twistings give the formulas of traditional creeds a different meaning (19). Obscure expressions in the Pauline writings are being misused (19; cf. 2 Pet. 3:16). The faithful are being mocked (cf. the " scoffers " of v. 18).

2. These doctrinal falsifications were coupled with a confusion

of morals. The false teachers were saying: everything is allowed, since sin that occurs in the flesh does not affect the spirit; on the contrary, it brings out the magnitude and glory of God's grace (cf. Rom. 6:1). God and world, spirit and matter, soul and body were being violently torn asunder. Hence the severity with which Jude condemns the moral conduct of the false teachers. Greed and incontinence are singled out as the clearest signs of their depravity. In their " ecstasy of freedom " they no longer pay any heed to moral law. They lead an unbridled life, turning the " new life " in Christ into its exact opposite. All this, Jude brings to light and threatens with divine retribution, so that it may alarm the faithful and serve the truth.

The letter of Jude is one of the first in a series of polemical writings against gnosis; the campaign was conducted not so much by dialogue and compromise as by outright rejection. Jude's readers were probably better served by this approach. The flat rejection is better understood when one takes into consideration the serious danger that threatened the very existence of the community. The whole Church was at stake. And yet the author of the letter was not a man who looked for trouble. His primary concern was the pastoral ministry. His letter was not written for professional theologians, but for the average Christian, who had to confront gnostics who were intellectually his superior. Pastoral concern is reflected in the instructions given the faithful on how to deal with those in error. Even the lukewarm are not despaired of; solicitude is demanded for them too (22, 23).

3. Gnosis attacks the Church's confession of faith. The preservation of Christianity entails holding fast to the truth handed down by the apostles as an inviolable, " most holy " treasure, given once and for all; it tolerates neither additions nor deletions. The letter of Jude recognizes the central characteristic of the faith entrusted to the Church: it was not a philosophy or a mytho-

logy but tradition that the historical Christ entrusted to his apostles and commissioned them to guard and to expound (cf. 1 Tim. 6:20; 2 Tim. 1:12, 14). This was to be a check on all human reinterpretation of divine revelation. Man must obediently accept what and how God has spoken and ordained. Only the man who renounces self-glorification can rise to such a decision.

Jude accuses the false teachers of being ungodly. They earn this appellation not because they deny the existence of a divine being, but because they do not reverence the God who reveals himself in the truth of faith handed down. The acceptance, in faith, of God's self-communication is not simply the assent of the intellect to a system of thought, but devotion to the living God who reveals himself to man in his great deeds in history. Only in faith and obedience does man escape self-imprisonment and attain to a genuine dedication to God—a dedication that is the goal of religion. If the false teachers are guilty of incontinence and greed, it only shows that they have not been able to rise above their own ego and therefore could not achieve true abandonment to God. Only the humble acceptance of the faith as it has been handed down to us can give direction, strength, and continuity to the Christian life.

OUTLINE

THE OPENING OF THE LETTER
(vv. 1 and 2)

In two lines, each consisting of two parts, the introductory greeting of the letter, in common New Testament usage, names the sender and the recipient (v. 1); there follows a threefold blessing (2).

The Sender (1a)

[1a]*Jude, a servant of Jesus Christ and brother of James . . .*

The author introduces himself as Jude, a servant of Jesus Christ. He is an apostle of Christ, someone no longer belonging to himself but assimilated to Jesus Christ, enlisted in his service and set at his disposal. Both the greatness and the smallness of the apostle is thereby expressed. He commands the highest authority, but speaks only in the service of Jesus Christ and under his authority. Jesus himself is heard in the preaching of his disciple. " He who hears you hears me, and he who rejects you rejects me " (Lk. 10:16). Jude is the brother of James. He thus identifies himself as the brother of the " brother of the Lord," highly respected in the Church, and head of the community at Jerusalem.

James, the brother of the Lord, underwent a martyr's death in the year 62. It is Jude's intention to continue with this letter his brother's apostolic work. The three designations—Jude, brother of James, apostle of Christ—are meant to win the author a respectful hearing. Behind him stand the primitive community at Jerusalem, the twelve apostles and Jesus Christ himself. The letter of Jude promises to be a witness to the tradition that goes back, through the Church and the persons who heard and saw him, to Jesus Christ.

The Destination of the Letter (1b)

¹ᵇ. . . *to those who are called, beloved in God the Father and kept for Jesus Christ.*

The letter is addressed to those who have been called; as one of the " catholic epistles," it is addressed to all Christians. All of us are its recipients. We are the ones whom God has called and chosen from among men. The source and accomplishment of our salvation was God's predilection of us and his calling us to become Christians.

God called us to salvation because he loved us. " God saved us and called us with a holy calling, not in virtue of our works but in virtue of his own purpose and the grace which he gave us in Christ Jesus ages ago " (2 Tim. 1:9). Christians are loved by God; from all eternity he has given them his love and he continually renews it. As Christians we are enveloped and protected in God's paternal love. It is the atmosphere in which we live and should live.

God has already wrought in us the essentials of our salvation. He has given us his love and it remains our gift; he has begun the work of keeping us for the perfecting of salvation, and his work remains operative in us. What God has already done for us through Jesus Christ founds our assurance that what he has begun he will bring to full realization.

In one way salvation is derived from God the Father, and in another way from Jesus Christ. It is the work of the Father, and then of the Son, for God acts in and through Jesus Christ.

Our confidence in God is grounded in Christ: in him we have all enrichment, because it pleased God to let the divine fullness reside in him. Even in this short introductory verse, something of this richness can be detected.

The Blessing (2)

²May mercy, peace, and love be multiplied to you.

Mercy, peace, and love are bestowed on believers by God. Jude presents these three gifts in an original way: they signalize for him the great reality of which the letter speaks and which is fundamental to Christianity. First the gracious gift of the Father is thought of as mercy. He has chosen us and called us—without any merit on our part. He has remitted all sin and dissolved all guilt. But we need his mercy continually, because we fail him continually. This is what we pray for every time we recite the " Our Father "; this is what we hope for in the final judgment.

The gift of God is also peace. The peace that the individual receives and experiences in himself is a sharing in the " great peace " that God has made with the world—by the work of atonement offered by his Son. If our sins are forgiven, then we enjoy the blessing of peace. All mankind is to be brought to a sharing in this peace, and so Jude expresses the wish that it be multiplied to us.

The greatest blessing is love, since it is God himself and comes from his heart to our own. " God's love has been poured into our hearts through the Holy Spirit which has been given to us " (Rom. 5:5). It is the surest foundation of our hope, the gift of consummation already present to us in our " pilgrim state," for love does not pass away even if all else passes away.

Salvation has already been given to us, but it must always be augmented. It is a kind of life; it seeks development and fruition. Only God can give an increase of mercy, peace, and love. Our wish and prayer are directed first of all and at their deepest to an increase of these blessings. We pray that they may be given us in their fullness.

THE BODY OF THE LETTER
(3–23)

Jude intended to write about the salvation offered to all men, but because false teachers had infiltrated the Church, he feels obliged to warn the faithful about them (3–16); he instructs them what they should do in face of this danger to the Church (17–23).

The Conduct of the False Teachers (3–16)

False teachers have gained admission to the Church (3–4). Even if they once were members in good standing, they are headed for perdition (5–7). Their conduct is exposed (8–13), and their condemnation in the coming judgment is threatened (14–16).

The Insidious Danger (3–4)

THE BATTLE SITUATION OF THE CHRISTIAN (3)

³*Beloved, being very eager to write to you of our common salvation, I found it necessary to write appealing to you to contend for the faith which was once for all delivered to the saints.*

The apostle's warning is prompted by love. It is because he loves the Christians that he warns them. He loves them because Christians are beloved, loved by God and by their fellow Christians, who are brothers to one another. Love is the climate in which Christian life thrives.

The Church and Jude its spokesman enthusiastically proclaim the wondrous salvation that God has prepared for us. Salvation is release from everything that oppresses man: sickness, misery, guilt, and death. " God will wipe away every tear from their eyes, and death shall be no more, neither shall there be mourning nor crying nor pain any more, for the former things have passed away " (Rev. 21:4). Salvation is everything that makes man happy. It gives " mercy, peace, and love "; it permits one to share in all that God has bestowed on his Son in exalting and glorifying him: resurrection, transfiguration, eternal life, and glory.

Salvation is offered to us all. In his graciousness, God wills to save all men, to give salvation to " the world," to re-create and renew the universe. The fullness of salvation begins with " the new earth and the new heaven."

Jude wanted to write a meditation on this gift of salvation, but he was obliged to compose an epistle against false teachers. It would be worth whatever effort it cost to steep oneself in the salvific truths of divine salvation, but falsehood is opposing the truth. The Church on earth cannot be only a church of contemplation; it must also be a church of militant action. Apostolic service in the life of the Church demands struggle—not one that need be sought out, but one that the nature of things imposes on us.

The field on which this battle must be fought is especially that of the faith that has been handed down once for all, the treasure of divine revelation. This great blessing has been entrusted to the saints. " Saints " are the Christians. God has chosen them from among other men, freed them from all sin, re-created them as new men, and put them in his service. By faith and baptism they are " the new Israel " which God has now endowed with the privileges he had promised to the Israel of old. Among those privileges was that of holiness. By baptism and by faith in the truth handed down, Christians are made holy, for sanctification takes place through obedience to the truth.

The faith that has been handed down bears the seal: once for all. God has spoken once for all. A tradition created by men has no comparable validity (Col. 2:8). The Church is not permitted to add anything to the teaching handed down, nor to delete anything from it. The whole of revelation is contained in that which has been handed down, for revelation was concluded in Jesus Christ. " In many and various ways God spoke of old to our fathers by the prophets; but in these last days he has spoken to us by a Son " (Heb. 1:1f.).

NEW APOSTLES (4)

'For admission has been secretly gained by some who long ago were designated for this condemnation, ungodly persons who pervert the grace of our God into licentiousness and deny our only Master and Lord, Jesus Christ.

The truth of faith is threatened. The new apostles and teachers were not " called " to their posts. They work anonymously (" some "), they have secretly gained admission into the community, they come as thieves. They have no authorisation in the community. Whoever takes upon himself a teaching role in the Church has to show that he has been so commissioned.

But God protects his revelation. Whoever does not speak by divine commission, but has stealthily entered the ranks of the teachers in the Church, will be punished by God. In the holy scriptures, God has in advance pronounced sentence on false teachers. Theirs is the condemnation that will be described in the following verses (5–7). Since they are ungodly, the condemnation of the ungodly applies to them. God has not decreed that they were to be ungodly, but that because they were so, they will not escape punishment.

The false teachers castigated by Jude pervert the grace of God into licentiousness. In their perversion, they use God's benevolent forgiveness as a pretext for sexual liberties. Perhaps they said to themselves, " Let us continue in sin that grace may abound " (Rom. 6:1).

The grace that God freely gives us is not a warrant for libertinism; it obliges us to a new life, a life according to grace. Baptism has remitted sin and showered God's favor and splendor on us; it therefore demands of us a life that reflects the radiant purity of its source. " You also must consider yourselves dead to sin and alive to God in Christ Jesus " (Rom. 6:11).

An unchaste life is a denial in practice that Jesus Christ is our " only Master and Lord." Even if Jesus is said to be the only Lord, he is denied by the deeds of the person who engages in unchaste actions. Jesus has won the right of possession over us. But the unchaste person abuses Christ's inheritance. As our divine Master, Jesus should command all our powers and faculties. As our powerful Lord, he also gives us the strength to restrain our inordinate desires.

Punishment (5–7)

The false teachers are convinced that they are saved. They think that baptism has guaranteed their salvation, and that therefore their moral conduct is irrelevant. In contrast, Jude cites three examples from the Old Testament to show that the salvation the Christian has received in baptism is absolute and final only if he holds fast to the confession of faith and leads a moral life that corresponds to his faith, in the acknowledgment of the lordship of Christ.

Death in the Wilderness (5)

⁵ᵃ*Now I desire to remind you, though you were once for all fully informed:*

He who professes the traditional faith of the Church is fully informed of all that concerns revelation and salvation. He has no need to learn " new truths " of faith—from heresiarchs. The person who proclaims something new contradicts the principle that the faith has been given once for all.

It is essential to the Christian life that the truths of faith be always operative and that they govern our conduct at all times. And therefore the basic law of all religious instruction takes the form: " I desire to remind you." In the holy scriptures we are reminded of the great deeds God has done for the salvation of men. In the same way, the preaching of the Church is intended to remind the faithful of what God has done.

⁵ᵇ*After the Lord had saved his people out of the land of Egypt, he destroyed those who did not believe.*

Israel's deliverance from Egypt is cited here as an instance of God's salvific intervention in Old Testament times. But were the Israelites definitively saved once they had been rescued from bondage? Not at all. God demanded of them a proof of their faith in the desert before they would be allowed to enter the promised land. The person who did not stand up to the test, but adjured the faith by murmuring against God, was condemned to die in the wilderness. Initially, God saved his people: he led them out of Egypt and they followed him; but a second time he let them perish, because they were remiss in faith and obedience. Their first salvation was not a guarantee of the second.

The Fall of the Angels (6)

⁶And the angels that did not keep their own position but left their proper dwelling have been kept by him in eternal chains in the nether gloom until the judgment of the great day.

God had endowed the angels with an exalted dignity; they exercised a celestial, princely authority and power. But some of them " did not keep their own position " in the celestial regions. Why? Jude takes for granted that the sin of these angels is well known (7). His remarks make it clear that for his mention of the fall of the angels he had in mind a mysterious book, not included in the Bible, the Book of Enoch.

The Genesis account of creation (Gen. 6: 12) narrates: " The sons of God saw that the daughters of men were fair; and they took to wife such of them as they chose." The Book of Enoch and other writings of the time interpreted " the sons of God " as angels. They were supposed to have left heaven, had intercourse with women and begotten giants. As punishment for this transgression they were consigned to " the nether gloom," jammed between sharp stones and kept like that until the time of the final judgment. At that time they will undergo their definitive punishment, which will take place in an immense pool of fire. So too according to the letter of Jude, the fallen angels are now undergoing only a preliminary punishment and will receive their definitive punishment in the final judgment.

The important point here is the warning that the text provides. God endowed the angels with majestic grandeur. But was this endowment irrevocable? Even the angels had to prove themselves. In infidelity, some of the angels forsook their rightful place—heaven—were rebellious to God, and therefore merited perdition.

THE FALL OF SODOM AND GOMORRAH (7)

*⁷Just as Sodom and Gomorrah and the surrounding cities, which
likewise acted immorally and indulged in unnatural lust, serve as
an example by undergoing a punishment of eternal fire.*

The fall of Sodom and Gomorrah and of the neighboring cities
Adma and Seboim is often mentioned in scripture as a divine
punishment. We should not forget what happened to them. All
God's deeds, including the times he had meted out punishment,
should be remembered by us.

The sin of these cities was unnatural lust. They were guilty of
incontinence and fornication. In the interpretation of the Old
Testament given here, the worst fault of the sinful cities was
that their inhabitants wanted to lay hold of the two angels who
had come as guests to Lot.

Redemption raises man to undreamed of heights. It gives the
people of God a wondrous freedom. The angels were invested
with glory; Sodom and Gomorrah prided themselves on their
opulence and splendor; we are the chosen and redeemed people
of the Lord—we share in the glory of Christ and are rich in
divine grace. Dare we now suppose that our hold on salvation
is unbreakable and we need not exert ourselves any further?
If we do not follow a conscience enlightened by the Holy Spirit,
if we misuse the grace of God—to say nothing of using it to
camouflage immorality—then perdition is our lot, despite our
having once been graced.

The threatened perdition that is imposed in the final judgment
is described as destruction, downfall, second death, eternal banish-
ment in gloom, eternal fire. These images, that speak of divine
punishment in human—and therefore inadequate—concepts and
terms give only a suggestion of the misery of the damned. Again
and again the irrevocability of their condemnation is referred to:
annihilation, timelessness, eternity.

Severe Accusations (8–13)

Remembrance of the three biblical punishments should have deterred the false teachers, but instead they commit the same sins of incontinence and presumption. They are shameless blasphemers (8–10), they pursue what the most reprobate sinners known to the Bible pursued (11), they are egotistic Pharisees (12–13). Each accusation against them is followed by a threat of punishment (10, 11, 13).

SHAMELESS BLASPHEMERS (8–10)

⁸*In like manner these men in their dreamings defile the flesh, reject authority, and revile the glorious ones.*

The false teachers are dreamers. The prophet Jeremiah names such persons false prophets, soothsayers, and diviners (Jer. 27–9). What they teach is not the truth that God has revealed, but a dream that emanates from a man. God's revelation is truth to which reality corresponds; a dream is the product of human fantasy, to which nothing corresponds.

But what these dreamers do is not harmless. " They defile the flesh." By their unchaste pursuits, their sexual excesses, they violate the sacred dignity of the Christian body. Not only the flesh—the exterior of man—is defiled, but the whole man, his mind and conscience (cf. Tit. 1 : 15). He who does not control passionate desire destroys the image of God in himself and withdraws his body from the service of Christ. " You were bought with a price. So glorify God in your body " (1 Cor. 6 : 20).

The false teachers " reject authority." Their immoral conduct stems from their rejection of Jesus Christ, whose authority they refuse to acknowledge. If they considered him their Lord, they could not act as they do. They have forgotten that they belong to him alone and have become " one spirit " with him.

They " revile the glorious ones." The angelic powers who surround God share in his glory. Even the fallen angels retain a degree of that glory, despite their fall; they are called " glorious ": " Bold and willful [men], they are not afraid to revile the glorious ones " (2 Pet. 2: 10b). The false teachers revile the fallen angels, for they consider them weaker than themselves; by their conduct they challenge the devil and want to probe " the deep things of Satan " (cf. Rev. 2: 24).

Defilement of the flesh, rejection of Christ's lordship, and revilement of the angelic world all have a common source: irreverence for God. Because they have no reverence for God, they ignore his revelation and fall victim to their own whims and dreams. They make themselves, not God, the center of their world, the norm of their judgments, the inspiration of their life. Instead of submitting to " the truth of faith handed down once for all," they assert their own self-glorification.

⁹*But when the archangel Michael, contending with the devil, disputed about the body of Moses, he did not presume to pronounce a reviling judgment upon him, but said, " The Lord rebuke you."*

Men presume to revile the glorious ones, the fallen angels. But Michael, whose name means " Who is like God " and who is the prince of the angels, did not dare to speak a condemnatory sentence on the devil, because he reverenced the glory of the angelic nature which even a fallen angel retains. Angels excel men in nature and glory, and—unlike some men—are filled with awe of God's creation.

The story to which Jude refers sounds odd to us. It is a Jewish legend that probably comes from the " Ascension of Moses " and gives an interpretation of the Old Testament passage: " He [Yahweh] buried Moses " (Deut. 34:6). His burial was also attributed to the angels. The legend embellishes the terse biblical text by picturing Michael and Satan contending for the corpse of Moses. The statement of divine condemnation is taken from the prophet Zechariah (Zech. 3:2).

[10]*But these men revile whatever they do not understand, and by those things that they know by instinct as irrational animals do, they are destroyed.*

In their blasphemous conduct, the false teachers boast of their knowledge (gnosis); they think themselves " knowing," " informed." But their blasphemies betray their ignorance. How could they mock had they real knowledge! It is not a higher knowledge that guides them, but their own unbridled nature with its instincts and drives. Mere nature does not empower one to understand celestial and spiritual things; for that, the Spirit and his supernatural inspiration are requisite. " God has revealed to us through the Spirit. For the Spirit searches everything, even the depths of God . . . The spiritual man judges all things, but is himself to be judged by no one " (1 Cor. 2:10, 15).

Warnings from the Old Testament (11)

[11]*Woe to them! For they walk in the way of Cain, and abandon themselves for the sake of gain to Balaam's error, and perish in Korah's rebellion.*

The " woe " of verse 11 applies to those who incur damnation, just as the " happy " of the beatitudes applies to those who will share in the kingdom of God and his glory (Mt. 5:3–10). Only in the last times is a definitive " woe " or " happy " spoken.

Cain was understood by Jude's contemporaries as the leader and guide of men who were given to revelry, thievery, and every kind of maliciousness; they were destined for perdition. The false teachers are doing what Cain did, and so they too are walking the same path to damnation as he walked.

Balaam was considered the prototype of the greedy man, the blasphemer, and the seducer. Just as he had led Israel into the trap of idol worship and licentiousness (Num. 31:16), the false teachers are leading the New Testament people of God into the sins of backsliding and debauchery. Like Balaam, the false teachers let themselves be carried away by avarice.

Korah's misdeed was to rebel against Moses and the Aaronite priesthood (Num. 16:1–35). He and his followers were destroyed by divine decree. Like Korah, the false teachers also resist Church authorities and rebel against serving God and the truth. They too are doomed to perdition, both now—because they have freely cut themselves off from the teaching handed down—and in the final judgment, when their fate will be sealed for eternity.

SMOKE WITHOUT FIRE (12–13)

¹²ᵃ*These are blemishes on your love feasts, as they boldly carouse together, looking after themselves; ...*

The celebration of the Eucharist in the early Church was held in conjunction with a banquet that is here called a love feast (*agape*). This expression gets directly to the heart of the eucharistic celebration. The Eucharist is the commemoration of the mystery of the Lord's death, the mystery of his love unto death. Only if it reflects this love is it fruitful. It is love that creates the atmosphere in which the Eucharist can be rightly understood and be salvific.

The false teachers take part in this holy meal, but they are blemishes on the sacred gathering because they fail in love. Boldly they feast with the community; for them the *agape* is only an opportunity for eating. It is not respect for the holy meal that motivates them, but the desire to eat. They profane the All Holy by their greed and they share in the holy meal unworthily because they are devoid of reverence for the mystery of the Lord's death.

They look after themselves. The true shepherd does not look after himself, but after his flock. The false teachers want to be shepherds, but their work is marred by self-seeking. They join in the celebration of the Eucharist, in which Christ in all self-lessness shows himself to be the true shepherd; but they think only of their own advantage. They completely reverse the law of life laid down by Christ—the law of love in the service of others. Any form of self-seeking or self-gratification is an out-right contradiction of the meaning of the Eucharist.

12b. . . *waterless clouds, carried along by winds; fruitless trees in late autumn, twice dead, uprooted;* . . .

No fruit is to be expected from the false teachers. Waterless clouds do not bring the rain that would make the earth fruitful; the fields lie parched and barren. After the harvest, trees in late autumn have nothing more to give that might sustain life. The false teachers enkindle hopes that can only be frustrated. Their teaching may well be new, interesting, ingenious; their manner of life may make an impression by its generous, " liberal," superior style. But in reality it is all froth and pretense; it cannot support life. Only the dry and sober truth does not disappoint.

The false teachers are twice dead, uprooted. They have died because they have separated themselves from the life giving truth; they have undergone a second death inasmuch as they are destined for the "second death" that is damnation. They are uprooted; they have forsaken the nourishing ground of truth. Only he who lives from the whole truth will receive life, bring forth fruit, and extend life to others.

[13]. . . *wild waves of the sea, casting up the foam of their own shame; wandering stars for whom the nether gloom of darkness has been reserved forever.*

Who can gauge and understand the rhythm of wild, storm-tossed waves? So too, the trajectories of meteors and comets (" wandering stars ") are at first sight irregular, unplotted, and unpredictable. Storm-waves and meteors exhibit great bursts of energy, but—according to the opinion of the time—they lack order and law. At its first appearance, a false doctrine often makes a greater show of vitality than orthodoxy can. But its " vitality " is not life; it is only " foam." Life is order; " vivaciousness " is activity without direction.

Threatened with Condemnation (14–16)

A prophecy of condemnation given in the apocryphal Book of Enoch is fulfilled in the false teachers (14–15); the text indicates the reason for their conduct (16).

THE PROPHECY OF JUDGMENT (14–15)

[14]*It was of these also that Enoch in the seventh generation from Adam prophesied, saying, " Behold, the Lord came with his holy myriads, [15]to execute judgment on all, and to convict all the ungodly of all their deeds of ungodliness which they have committed in such an ungodly way, and of all the harsh things which ungodly sinners have spoken against him."*

Jude cites, with considerable freedom, a passage from the Book of Enoch. The actual passage reads: " And see, he [God] comes with myriads of the saints, to execute judgment on all, and he will annihilate the ungodly and reprimand all flesh because of all the ungodly deeds that the ungodly have committed, and because of all the harsh words they have spoken and because of all the evil they have spoken about him." Enoch is referred to as the seventh from Adam because he stands seventh in the row of the patriarchs (Gen. 5: 18). There are mysterious intimations that he led a holy life, dedicated to God: " He walked with God." He was the only one among the patriarchs to be taken up suddenly by God: " Enoch walked with God; and [suddenly] he was not [any longer there], for God took him " (cf. Gen. 5: 22–24). He was considered an intimate of God who learned hidden truths, especially as regards the " last things." The book that bore his name was held in great reverence. Jude does not hesitate to quote a passage from it. Everything it says about divine judgment is in conformity with what the holy scriptures say on the same subject. It is an example of how broad-minded one could be even in the apostolic age, so long as the truth was proclaimed.

The Lord will come. For Jude, the Lord is Christ. In the language of the prophets it was said: " The Lord has come." His coming is so certain that it is viewed as a phenomenon of the past. Because of the certainty of future events, the prophets spoke of them as if they had already taken place. The word of the Lord does not deceive; history, as a timeless presence, lies open to its view.

The revelation especially under consideration here is that of judgment. All deeds and words will be submitted to judgment. Do the false prophets hope that they will be spared? May the baptized person think himself safe because of his baptism? Does he think he will not be judged? The word ungodly is used four times. The false teachers are described as ungodly revilers. They are the ones who are threatened with judgment. When the glory of God is revealed in judgment, when the myriads of angels proclaim the majesty of the Lord, what will these revilers say then? Only in the light of this judgment do we see with perfect clarity. It should engender in us a holy and salutary fear.

UNGODLY SINNERS (16)

[16a]*These are grumblers, malcontents, following their own passions, . . .*

Grumbling comes from the rejection of God in disbelief. The Jews complained during the wandering in the desert, the contemporaries of Jesus murmured when he spoke of bread from heaven, the day laborers grumbled when they were paid what they were owed but less than what they were expecting. The false teachers are not content with the truth handed down; they are dissatisfied with God. They think they know better; they feel themselves restricted and patronized.

They follow their own passions, giving in to incontinence and greed. They boast that total redemption is theirs and therefore they are totally free; giving in to passion will not disturb their conviction of definitive redemption. But did not their conscience reproach them when they allowed themselves to be led by passion? Did not their grumbling against God come from an awareness that they were living a contradiction within themselves? They were out of sorts with themselves because they believed they had already won consummate redemption, whereas it is only promised as a future possibility.

[16b] *. . . loud-mouthed boasters, flattering people to gain advantage.*

The heresiarchs are guilty of haughty and blasphemous speech; they are ready to instruct God and to point out his mistakes. Their grumbling and loud-mouthed boasting have a common source. The false teachers set themselves up as the norm for God; they will not submit to the teaching guaranteed by tradition. They flatter people, patronizing the great and powerful, for their own advantage. Their attitude to others is not inspired by respect and love, but by avarice and egotism.

Greed distorts everything; it inveigles men and leads to rebellion against God. It dethrones God and makes men slaves. How can the man who acknowledges only himself have genuine respect for the revealed word of God?

Duties of the Faithful (17–23)

The letter turns now to the loyal believers. They are wrestling with the question: Why does God tolerate the heresiarchs, who endanger the Church? The faithful are not to wonder about the advent of false teachers nor to take offense at them, for it was all foretold by the apostles (17). The apostolic teaching expressly mentions them (18) and they show all the signs predicted of them (19). In this time of danger the faithful must lead a more intensive spiritual life (20–21); their concern for the errant must search out the right stance to maintain in their regard (22–23).

Why False Teachers? (17–19)

¹⁷*But you must remember, beloved, the predictions of the apostles of our Lord Jesus Christ; . . .*

Believers live in love. In his loving care for them, God has made provision to protect them from going astray when false teachers appear on the scene. Forewarned is forearmed.

The apostles have spoken in advance about the coming of false teachers. Paul, in his moving farewell address in Miletus, said that ravenous wolves would break into the Church and would lead some away. In his pastoral epistles he relates how the Spirit has said that false teachers would bring about the downfall of many in the last times. The prophecy of the apostles is an echo of Jesus' prophecy that false messiahs and false prophets would appear in the last times. This is one of the trials that God ordains the Church should undergo.

[18]*They said to you, " In the last time there will be scoffers, following their own ungodly passions."*

The false teachers are called scoffers. It is not that they mock particular teachings and opinions of the Church, but rather they reject God's revelations *in toto.* Those who feared God have always been harassed by scoffers. Christ himself was exposed to them in his passion. Scoffing comes from self-exaltation, from the supposed superiority of the scoffer's own judgment. One can be deeply wounded by it, especially one who tries to accept the kingdom of God as candidly as a child, in sheer devotion and eagerness. Even in the Church, many will make fun of this and deride it as naïve simplicity.

The advent and activities of the false teachers indicated to the early Church that the end time had begun. As long as this era perdures, there will always be false teachers. It is one form of Satan's struggle against God's royal dominion. If one's thinking is confused, how soon one's actions will follow suit: " They follow their own ungodly passions." The history of the Church provides many examples.

¹⁹It is these who set up divisions, worldly people, devoid of the Spirit.

The heresiarchs tried to deduce their teachings from traditional doctrine. They were very pleased with their cleverness. They contrast one concept with another, find different meanings, campaign with empty words—and would thus insinuate their ideas into the deposit of faith. But only in the stream of apostolic tradition confirmed by the unanimous witness of each age can religious concepts retain the meaning that God has willed.

Building Up the Life of Religion (20, 21)

²⁰But you, beloved, build yourselves up on your most holy faith; pray in the Holy Spirit; ²¹keep yourselves in the love of God; wait for the mercy of our Lord Jesus Christ unto eternal life.

The faithful are to build themselves up to the closely knit structure that is the Church. One member supports and strengthens the other, does what he can to contribute to the compactness and security of the body collective. From the community, the individual gains new strength.

The fundament of the spiritual structuring of the Church is the truth of faith, here solemnly called "your most holy faith." If the truth of faith is no longer confessed in its fullness, then the unity and strength of the whole structure is threatened. Faithfully holding fast to the traditional truth supports the faith of others. What God has given us we must keep inviolable and revered.

Faith in action takes especially the form of prayer. Christian prayer is inspired by the Holy Spirit. " You have received the spirit of sonship, in which we cry, ' Abba! Father ' " (Rom.

8 : 15). " The Spirit helps us in our weakness; for we do not know how to pray as we ought, but the Spirit himself intercedes for us with sighs too deep for words " (Rom. 8 : 26).

Keep yourselves in the love of God. God has lavishly bestowed his love on us. To conserve it, we must prove it again and again. If faith is expressed in prayer, it will prove itself in life and love. Prayer in the Holy Spirit teaches the Christian that God is his father, that he lives in the paternal love of God and therefore must keep his law, in love. The law of the Spirit is our love of God and of the children of God.

The Christian lives in the expectation of the return of the Lord in judgment. Our attitude is not only that of fear of judgment —which the letter has also intended to arouse—but the confident expectation that our Lord Jesus Christ will exercise mercy. Even the just man would not be acquitted if the judge rendered judgment only according to strict justice, not tempered by mercy. Only the mercy of Jesus Christ can open for us the door to eternal life.

All that we do should be an expression of love. " Keep yourselves in love " is the central thought of the verse; everything else " participates " in love: perseverance in the faith, prayer in the Spirit, hope for mercy in the final age.

Attitude towards Those in Error (22–23)

[22]*And convince some, who doubt;* [23]*save some, by snatching them out of the fire; on some have mercy with fear, hating even the garment spotted by the flesh.*

Many, because of the work of the heresiarchs, have become doubters. They have not yet turned entirely away from the apostolic truth and decided utterly for heresy. They are to be shown the right way and convinced by the truth. This monitum is directed to all the faithful. Love—of which they are reminded by the salutation " Beloved " (20)—lays upon them the duty of concern for those in danger.

The second group have already fallen victim to the false teaching and are therefore already consigned to the fire of punishment. If they are not converted, they will certainly suffer damnation. The faithful are to help these people also. " Save them! Snatch them from the fire!" Their need is great, but there is still reason to hope that their conversion is possible.

The third group have so assimilated the false teaching that they cannot now be won back. But even to them, one should show mercy. It might take the form of supplicatory prayer, or some other expression of sympathy fostered by love and concern for their salvation. " You should not hate anyone, but correct some, pray for others, and others love more than your own soul."

Mercy must be joined to fear of defilement and contagion. What are the faithful to do? In graphic terms, they are told they must hate the very garments that the false teachers wear. Even proximity to them can have a contagious and perverting effect and therefore all exterior contact with them, and even physical nearness, must be avoided. They are " worldly," victims of sin, shut off from the Holy Spirit. As human beings, they are to be treated mercifully, but there is not to be any backsliding when it comes to a question of truth. Love must be circumspect and prudent lest, while trying to save others, love itself be led to destruction.

THE CLOSING OF THE LETTER
(24–25)

The letter closes without any personal remark or greeting, but
with a solemn hymn of praise. The vilifications of the ungodly,
so often referred to, are countered by an expression of veneration
and worship of God. It is the answer of faith to the God of truth.

*[24]Now to him who is able to keep you from falling and to present
you without blemish before the presence of his glory with rejoic-
ing, [25]to the only God, our Saviour through Jesus Christ our Lord
be glory, majesty, dominion, and authority, before all time and
now and forever. Amen.*

The first phrase lauds the divine power. The fulfillment of our
prayers of petition is founded on God's power. This power is
revealed especially by his gift of salvation. We will attain it only
if God keeps us from falling and sets us, without moral blemish,
before his face. Only God can strengthen us to bear the radiance
of his holiness.

God sets us before the presence of his glory. What a striking
image! God will reveal himself without restriction; we are permitted to see him as he is. As the pious Jews rejoiced when
they experienced the nearness of God's glory in the temple, so he
who shares in the joy of the final epoch will rejoice, but more so.
There will be a liturgy in which " hearing and seeing " will
have no place—something we, from such a distance, can hardly
imagine now. The celebration of the liturgy on earth can only be
a weak foretaste of the eternal celebration in heaven.

The doxology is addressed to the one God and Saviour. God
is the absolutely unique being, with whom no creature can be
compared. He is the Saviour, because all salvation comes from

him. But he accomplishes his salvation through Jesus Christ, our Lord. Jesus is the mediator of all God's works—creation, revelation, reconciliation, judgment, and consummation. Our way to the Father leads through Jesus Christ; he is the door.

We can proclaim the praise of God only by telling others, in our stumbling way, what we have experienced of him and what we in our experience have learned. Four such statements are included here. To God belongs glory, the might and radiance in which God reveals himself in his manifestations to us. To him belongs majesty, supremacy, excellence over all else. God has dominion—over all created being. Nothing can withstand him; ultimate victory is his. God has authority; in his supreme freedom he disposes over his work and his creation.

All this is true of God for all eternity. We can think of eternity only in temporal terms, as that which has neither beginning nor end. Everything attributed to God is true of him equally in the past, the present, and the future. The fullness of being is eternally his.

" Amen, so be it " is the answer of the people to the words of the prayer leader. The faithful agree to the praise given to God and make it their own. When the Church proclaims the praise of God's glory, it finds an echo in the Amen of the faithful.

The false teaching of the heresiarchs is not entirely unsuccessful, but the faithful should not lose heart. The Church lives from the mighty works of God. He is the Saviour and Redeemer through the Lord Jesus Christ. Victory belongs to God. In his glory, exaltation, power, and authority we are protected and kept for eternal life. The militant tone and language of the letter up to this point ends with the solemn and sacred tones of veneration, in the confidence that, despite whatever reverses and weaknesses, God will conduct us to the beatific vision of his glory. We assent to this way of the Church that leads through battle to the effulgent glory of God; it is our way through life in the worshipful veneration of our " Amen."